SUBJECTIVE MEANING AND CULTURE:
An Assessment Through
Word Associations

Lorand B. Szalay
INSTITUTE OF COMPARATIVE SOCIAL
AND CULTURAL STUDIES, INC.
WASHINGTON, D.C.

James Deese
UNIVERSITY OF VIRGINIA

 LAWRENCE ERLBAUM ASSOCIATES, PUBLISHERS
1978   Hillsdale, New Jersey

DISTRIBUTED BY THE HALSTED PRESS DIVISION OF
JOHN WILEY & SONS
New York   Toronto   London   Sydney

Lawrence Erlbaum Associates, Inc., Publishers
62 Maria Drive
Hillsdale, New Jersey 07642

Distributed solely by Halsted Press Division
John Wiley & Sons, Inc., New York

Library of Congress Cataloging in Publication Data
Szalay, Lorand B.
 Subjective meaning and culture.

 Bibliography: p.
 Includes indexes.
 1. Meaning (Psychology)—Testing. 2. Subjectivity—
Testing. 3. Cross-cultural studies—Testing.
4. Association tests. I. Deese, James Earle, 1921–
joint author. II. Title.
BF463.M4S9   155.28′4   78-15561
ISBN 0-470-26486-1

Printed in the United States of America

Contents

020355

Preface

In this volume we present a framework and a method for the comparative study of the perceptions, attitudes, and cultural frames of reference shared by groups of people. Our framework is the notion of subjective meaning, and our method is that of word associations. We present a detailed account of some particular cross-cultural and intergroup comparisons using the word-association technique described in this volume. However, we do not wish to emphasize comparisons but rather the technique itself as a method in the investigation of subjective meaning and with it subjective culture. Our purpose, then, is to introduce a research capability which offers new kinds of information and makes critical aspects of subjective meaning accessible to empirical investigation.

While the technology of communication has progressed at a phenomenal rate, advances in the human aspects of communication are disappointingly small. We can transmit a television image around the world, but there have been no comparable advances in reducing psychological distance among peoples, in promoting mutual understanding, in acquiring and using knowledge necessary for the bridging of cultural differences, in being able to relate to others in terms of their meanings and experiences. Perhaps, by their nature, such advances in the human sciences are slow and difficult. We hope that the method presented in this book will make a useful contribution toward achieving these goals.

From a psychological point of view, communicating is largely a matter of knowing what themes are important to people and addressing those themes in ways that accord with the subjective meaning people attach to them. While subjective meaning and, most importantly, priorities in subjective meaning are personal and often inaccessible to the outsider, free associations have the unique potential for penetrating the world of subjective meaning.

The potential for word associations to reveal the mental content of our subjective world has been recognized by thinkers from Plato to Freud, but the exploitation of this potential has been hampered by deceptive preconceptions about the nature of associations as well as by the limitations of earlier methods.

Some of the preconceptions come out of psychological theory. So-called association theory and the classical "laws of association" have prevented many psychologists from seeing the full potential for associations to reveal the inner world. The layman has often been less blinded. It is easy for the average person to see that associations do reveal inner relations. He can see that freedom is a promise to the oppressed and a threat to the tyrant, that transportation to an American is a car or a jet, to a Bedouin a camel.

But there are other preconceptions that the psychologist and the layman share. One is that associations are commonplace and trivial. Another is that they are erratic and whimsical. We can, however, in comparing our own commonplace associations with those of people from other cultures, become aware of the fact that these apparently commonplace and trivial associations reveal profound aspects of our subjective culture and how that culture differs from the culture of others.

Associations are not erratic and whimsical. They are stable, and they relate clearly and naturally to our experiences. They are organized and structured just as are our perceptions, beliefs, and attitudes. In fact, associations reflect the structure of perceptions, beliefs, and attitudes.

The particular technique used in most of the comparative studies performed by Szalay and his associates is called associative group analysis. The results of these studies support the notions introduced by Deese in his concept of associative meaning. Associative group analysis focuses upon those aspects of subjective meaning common to members of a group rather than upon those unique to individuals. In this volume we have placed associative group analysis in the more general framework of the study of association, but the primary group comparisons.

Chapter 1 presents the theory relating subjective meaning and word associations. We assume that word associations allow us to reconstruct subjective meaning. While word associations also reflect the lexical meaning, more importantly they reveal perceptions and attitudes. It is this aspect of the distributions of word associations that causes us to use the term subjective or psychological meaning and to argue that it is more than linguistic meaning. Since subjective meaning is frequently below the level of awareness, it cannot always be verbalized or communicated in response to direct questions. For reasons pointed out in Chapter 1, free associations reveal understanding at a deeper level than would be conveyed by a definitive statement or response to a particular question. Distributions of responses characterize the general subjective meaning shared by groups or cultures, and comparison of distributions of responses reveals differences in group thinking, perception, and attitudes.

It is possible, by examining consistent group priorities revealed by responses to particular themes and domains, to reconstruct the subjective representational system that characterizes a group. The representational system provides the particular cultural frame of reference for a group. The characterization of such a cultural frame of reference requires a particular strategy in the selection of stimuli to be used in free association, and this question receives only a passing treatment in this volume. The primary focus of the present volume is instead upon illustrating the use of distributions of free associations to infer subjective meaning.

An important characteristic of associative analysis is that it minimizes intervention by the investigator. It does not rely on questioning or scaling, and it is relatively free, except in the selection of stimuli, from the rationalizations and preconceptions of the investigator. Even here, techniques exist to select stimuli so that they are representative of the significant themes in a culture and not the investigator's preconceptions.

We are mindful that there is a certain skepticism about the use of free associations to infer subjective meaning, and we have in many places throughout this volume explained what it is that gives free associations their unique ability to probe the important and affectively significant relationships in people's lives.

We are indebted to many agencies which have supported the work upon which this book is based, and we recognize the collaboration and assistance of many persons in carrying out the work. Among the agencies and institutions which have supported this work are: National Institute of Mental Health; U. S. Office of Education, Division of International Education; Department of the Navy; Advanced Research Projects Agency; Philosophical Society; and the National Science Foundation. The authors express their sincere gratitude and appreciation to the numerous colleagues, coauthors, and work associates who made important contributions to the present volume. To mention a few: Roy D'Andrade, University of California; Bela Maday, National Institute of Mental Health; Rita Kelly and Vincent Kelly of Rutgers University; Robert E. Williams, University of the District of Columbia; Ralph K. White, George Washington University; Jack Brent, UNICOR, Department of Justice; Ralph Swisher, LEAA, Department of Justice; Norman Smith, American Insitutes for Research; Dale Lysne, American Institutes for Research; Margret Brena, Institute of Comparative Social and Cultural Studies; John Kringen, University of Maryland; Charles Windle, National Institute of Mental Health; Garmon West, Howard University; Hilda Wing, U. S. Civil Service Commission; Alyssa McCabe and Cassendra Wright, University of Virginia. Among the various contributors listed or unmentioned, the valuable and continuous assistance and contributions offered by Jean Bryson Strohl through her interest and dedication deserve separate recognition.

LORAND B. SZALAY
JAMES DEESE

1

Psychological Meaning and the Associative Method

The notion of meaning is viewed differently by different disciplines. The linguist, the philosopher, and the psychologist each views the concept in some unique way, though all agree that meaning is a kind of relation, as Ogden and Richards (1923/1956) first pointed out, among mind, object, and word. The differences in viewpoint come down to what pair of terms in this triadic relation are emphasized. The interest of the linguist, for example, centers on what might be called *lexical meaning*, the conventional and arbitrary relation between a word and its referent.

LEXICAL AND REFERENTIAL MEANING

The basis of lexical meaning is convention. It operates as a broad and tacit agreement, as a collective force connecting words with objects and categories of objects. This convention, a collective code of labeling, has its roots in the use of language by countless individuals — in their habits of language and in their correlated mental processes. Linguists do not deny individual variations in use, but they generally disregard them. Although each linguistic act has some individuality and each use of language has its foundation in subjective psychological processes, linguistic interest begins at the level of the shared, the collective rules, the conventional. Thus, for lexicography, users of a language count as individuals only to the extent that they represent the collective and that their behavior conforms to, and informs about, the conventional. Bloomfield (1933) justified the linguist's omission of the individual by stressing the importance of definitions as reflections of collective agreement: "If he (the individual speaker) has not

1

heard it (the word) very many times, or if he has heard it under very unusual circumstances, his use (meaning) of the word may deviate from the conventional. We combat such personal deviations by giving explicit definitions of meaning: this is the chief use of our dictionaries" (p. 152).

This limitation affects the practical utility of the concept of lexical meaning only where lexical meaning is misconstrued to represent subjective meaning. Naturally, lexical meaning is inappropriate for application to psychological processes in individual human beings.

The philosophical or rational concern with meaning centers on the concept—referent relation. It is this relation that has so occupied the attention of contemporary theorists. Since the rise of generative theory, almost every serious treatment of meaning has centered on this relation (e.g., Katz, 1972), and despite the use of such theory in models of human memory and the like (e.g., Kintsch, 1974), the relation is essentially rational and logical in nature. In this treatment, meaning becomes synonymous with rational knowledge. This synonymity leads to an epistemological interest in meaning and concern with problems intrinsic to the acquisition of knowledge.

These notions, lexical and referential meaning, emphasize the arbitrary nature of the relation between word and referent. Despite the essential correctness of such a point of view, it can lead to the wrong conclusion. It produces a strong disposition to forget about the human organism's highly interdependent and not necessarily logical system of semantic habits and representations. These semantic habits interact with the structure of language in a complex way, for in language words are not created as arbitrarily as it might appear. Words with related meaning often derive from common roots, and the predispositions created in people by these semantic affinities represent powerful psychological forces operating beyond the level of awareness. Some concepts are psychologically more important or controlled than others. The less the speaker is aware of such semantic affinities, the greater their potential for influence.

PSYCHOLOGICAL MEANING

Psychological meaning describes a person's subjective perception and affective reactions to segments of language. It characterizes those things that are most salient in an individual's reactions and describes the degree and direction of affectivity. In comparison, rational or philosophical meaning describes the abstract characteristics of the referent and its relation with other conceivable referents, while lexical meaning describes the dyadic relations between words and referents. These are all, to be sure, interrelated, but it is possible, and indeed even necessary, to concentrate on one or the other aspects of meaning in order to understand certain problems. In the balance of this book, we are primarily concerned with psychological meaning.

The Notion of Mediation

The psychological study of meaning has been chiefly empirical. What theory there is arises out of a kind of neobehaviorism. Osgood (1952), of course, is the person, who, more than anyone else, has championed the psychological study of meaning through his famous semantic differential. Although Osgood's predecessors are not all behaviorists — after all both Wundt and Titchener espoused a process view of psychological meaning — his chief roots are in behaviorism. The incipient fractional response theory of meaning, which lies at the bottom of the conceptual framework of the semantic differential, has its origins in Watson (1924) and his demonstration that thought processes are correlated with small, incipient movements of the vocal organs. The notion of response mediation, which provides the theoretical background of the semantic differential, owes more to Hull (1930) than to Watson, however. Hull's notion of the pure stimulus act arises from the proprioceptive consequences of responses and leads directly to the notion of mediation. It is the concept of mediation that is responsible for the behavioristic notion of psychological meaning.

The concept of mediation became particularly popular with neobehaviorists because it allowed them to deal with and "explain" cognitive processes by conceiving of them as mediating chains with one or more covert links. Osgood (1952) described the meaning as a covert coding reaction that is both mediational and representational in nature. The recognition of these two aspects of meaning gives Osgood's notion considerable flexibility. Both Osgood and more recent cognitive theorists agree that meaning has a mediating and a representational function. This difference is one of emphasis, with cognitive theorists being much more concerned with representation. Osgood placed particular emphasis on the fact that psychological meaning is a reaction of the human organism, a reaction subject to rules and controlled by characteristic dispositions. He emphasized that psychological meaning constitutes, in the final analysis, a neural process and that we know practically nothing about its neurophysiology. Osgood (1964) cogently argued, however, that it is compelling to assume that meaning consists of a bundle of components: "The meaning of a sign is conceived to be a simultaneous bundle of distinctive semantic features — which identify with component r's of the total r_m" (p. 403). These components represent the main constituents of the person's understanding and evaluation of the word (that is, its referent). They may represent experiences, images, and feelings about the word (that is, its referent), accumulated directly or vicariously in the past.

Background for the Present Method

The background for the investigations reported in this book shares some of this view, but places it in a broader perspective. The main practical departure is in the rejection of the fixed-response format associated with the semantic differential and its replacement by a method of free responding consistent with the propositional notion presented later. We may begin with the common experience that meaning as a subjective reaction involves the person's actual understanding, perception, and evaluation, even though certain elements of this understanding are necessarily vague, ambiguous, and not readily communicable. The psychological meaning of a concept such as "war" for a professional soldier may include, for instance, such components as "military strategy," "victory," "order of battle," "combat training," and "image of enemy." For a civilian, components such as "H-bomb," "radiation," and "fear" may be particularly strong. One may object that radiation, its biogenetic effects and other things, do not, in a logical sense, constitute parts of war; they are merely consequences of it. Yet important consequences and their anticipation appear to be potent components of a system of subjective meaning. The understanding of the subjective meaning of war is not the same for those who look forward to victory as for those who anticipate fatal radiation effects.

Our interest in the behavioral implications of subjective meaning underlines the importance of certain components that lie beyond the framework of a logical meaning. In the control of goal-oriented human behavior by subjective meaning, components such as those involving anticipated consequences are of particular importance. Anticipated consequences do influence our behavior. The anticipated consequences of war influence what position people are inclined to take, what alternative action they will choose, whether they will fight or demonstrate, whether they will go to combat, to exile, or to jail.

Although this point has been made before by psychologists ranging from Titchener to Osgood, there is a strong and general inclination to fall back upon purely linguistic and logical categories. Logical and linguistic analysis creates a natural disposition to neglect what is important in psychological meaning, the fact that certain components are more central to the psychological representation than others and the fact that the whole of psychological meaning is suffused with affectivity.

This disposition is responsible for the failure of certain direct elicitation techniques or detailed linguistic analysis to reveal components of subjective or psychological meaning. Direct questions about what words mean lead to explication often in the form of part—whole relations, superordinate categories, or other linguistically relevant relations. Psychological aspects of the reactions persons have to words and the concepts behind words are systematically disregarded. If we are to learn something about the structure of subjective meaning, we need to do what Osgood (1952) and Deese (1965) have done, namely to conceive of a meaningful reaction as being the aggregate of component reactions and potential component reactions irrespective of their linguistic or logical status. Thus, the subjective meaning of "war," can be approximated by listing the potential component reactions: R_1 "fight," R_2 "killing," R_3 "fear," R_4 "enemy," R_5 "victory," R_6 "strategy," R_7 "patriotism," R_8 "military," etc.

There is considerable, but inescapable, arbitrariness in the labeling by which we try to identify and to communicate about the subjective meaning reaction and its components. When we list "enemy" as a component of our meaning of "war," we do not mean "enemy" literally, but merely use it as a label to stand for the specific referent — the specific image in the mind as to the most probable adversary, a particular world power, probably armed with nuclear weapons, viewed as representing the greatest threat, the danger of aggression. Again, although logically "war" and "enemy" are separate concepts, our psychological meaning of war will differ depending on whether the "enemy" is vague and uncertain or a particular strong and aggressive power. Viewing psychological meaning as a collection of such components means that we do not differentiate among those components that have linguistic and logical status, such as "fight" and "killing," and those that do not, such as "fear" and "victory."

Psychological meaning is naturally subject to the rules that characterize the dynamic interaction between external stimuli and the internal states or dispositions of the person. Of these, focusing and selectivity seem particularly important. The meaning reaction is focused and highly selective. A few components will play roles of critical importance, while a broad variety of objective characteristics of the referent will receive little, if any, representation. "War," "military strategy" and "combat training" will probably be components with high salience (high priority and intensive attention) for an officer but may play a negligible role for a draft evader. This implies that, rather than assuming that many components have equal weight, we should distinguish between more and less salient ones.

The practical importance of salience is obvious when we recognize that logically one can differentiate between essential and accidental characteristics and that the number of intellectually applicable characteristics in any given case is nearly astronomical. A small random sample shows that nearly 80% of the adjectives offered by *Webster's Collegiate Dictionary* can be used to characterize war, particularly if we allow for metaphoric and synesthetic use. Yet, both because components tend to covary and because certain components are more salient than others, a small number of words may characterize quite accurately the meaningful reactions that a large number of people have to a given concept.

Although in a lexical or logical analysis the salience of characteristics is generally beyond the scope of consideration, in the study of psychological meaning it has unique importance. As we will see in numerous examples, the meanings held by individuals and groups rarely differ in an absolute qualitative sense but often differ quantitatively in the salience of their components. The meanings of "war" to the officer and the draft evader will be similar in intellectually applicable characteristics. Intellectually, the draft evader will agree that war has to do with military strategy and the officer that in war innocent people are killed. They will, nevertheless, have different psychological meanings, based in part on the different degrees of dominance they assign to these components.

Compared with lexical meaning, psychological meaning is unstable and labile. The degree of instability varies with the nature of the referent. The meaning of "hunger" probably shows some periodic fluctuations over short periods of time as we are sated or hungry. Other changes are slower and less periodic but may still be extensive and dramatic. Moods, needs, external events, impressions, and direct and vicarious experiences all subject our psychological reactions to concepts to much greater variation than ordinary lexical meaning allows.

THE STUDY OF PSYCHOLOGICAL MEANING

There are two major strategies for attacking the problem of psychological meaning, both of which depend upon the analysis of verbal reactions. The first strategy is direct. It focuses on single words and aims to identify the major components of the reactions to concepts by scaling or some other method. The classical technique here, of course, is the semantic differential. The second strategy is indirect. It examines the interrelations among words within groups and clusters. Multidimensional scaling of similarity judgments is the best known technique developed to date (see Fillenbaum & Rapoport, 1971).

Fixed-Response Methods

The first strategy can also allow for an important variation in the mode of responding. The reactions of a person may be determined by asking him to respond by picking an item from a fixed number of alternatives or by rating a concept on some labeled scale as in the semantic differential. But it is also possible to allow the individual to respond freely, as in the use of associative data to investigate psychological meaning (Deese, 1965). This is particularly important as we try to move away from "mere words" and concentrate on the propositions revealed by relations *between* words, as in free associations. These, in turn, reveal the psychological representation of meaning.

The semantic differential, first introduced by Osgood in 1952, is overwhelmingly the best-known research technique for the investigation of psychological meaning. It asks people to rate concepts on a set of scales. The scales, which usually have a 7-point range, extend from one adjective to its opposite. Thus, on a semantic differential, people will be asked to rate a concept such as "war" on scales anchored by good–bad, strong–weak, etc. If the results are to be employed in a direct strategy, it is possible to produce the semantic composition of a concept by showing its semantic profile. Or, it is possible to use an indirect approach by subjecting the semantic profiles of a set of concepts to some multivariate technique that extracts the principal components. The relations among these concepts may then be displayed in some n-dimensional semantic space.

In its most widely used form, the semantic differential consists of about 20 scales. According to the original guidelines, the scales were to be selected specifically in terms of the subject of study, but the search for an instrument of universal applicability has led to an increasing preference for standard scales. These scales focus mostly on evaluation (good–bad, pleasant–unpleasant) and, to a lesser extent, on potency (strong–weak) and activity (fast–slow), and when employed in an indirect strategy, the results are usually displayed in a space having the three independent dimensions of evaluation, potency, and activity. Osgood, in many places, has argued that these dimensions are universal to psychological meaning, that we always react to concepts in these ways. He is probably right, but the problem is that we also react to concepts in very specific ways that often cannot be predicted ahead of time, so that it is impossible to design a priori a set of scales that will tap the appropriate reaction to the more specific and hence cross-culturally interesting aspects of meaning.

Finding scales relevant to a single meaning is a demanding task. Finding scales relevant to the study and comparison of reactions of diverse composition is even more demanding. Finding a single set of scales of universal applicability, a scale set bearing on the salient components of all meaning, reduces all psychological meaning to some gross oversimplification. A compromise may be sought in two directions. One is to adhere to the requirement of relevance of the scales and to use scales that bear on a single selected domain of concepts. The other is to persist in the goal of finding a universal instrument. The majority of investigations of meaning using the semantic differential have moved in this second direction. Thus, the specificity of scales and the strategy of the direct reproduction of meaning through semantic profiles receive little attention from the users of this instrument.

Strategies with Fixed-Response Methods

Most of those who have looked for specificity have tended to employ a different strategy. They have attempted to map some local region of "semantic space" by studying the relationships among the terms of some limited semantic field through similarity judgments. The most widely used method for constructing these relations relies upon judgments of similarity among three words presented in all possible combinations. The triads are made up of a reference word and two words from which the respondent is to pick the one that is more similar to the reference word. The number of choices made by a number of subjects provides the quantitative basis for the calculations.

As Miller (1967) pointed out, the difficulty that such a procedure faces is that "a truly enormous amount of data is required" (p. 41). To study some large semantic field with these techniques is almost impossible. Stefflre and his associates (Stefflre, Reich, & McClaren-Stefflre, 1971) have tried to get around this problem simply by counting the incidence of common contexts, and Szalay

(1961) has employed the even simpler procedure of tabulating the frequency of similarity judgments.

The popularity of this general strategy has several roots. Whether or not it is explicit, the judgment of relationship between words is based on subjective meaning reaction and represents a spontaneous choice controlled by salient components of perception and evaluation. This judgment may be little affected by lexical or logical considerations. It seems automatically to adapt to and account for the natural salience of meaning components, whereas introspective efforts to identify and convey the salience of meaning components can lead to biased results. Furthermore, it is much easier to elicit spontaneous choices in such tasks than it is to elicit definitions or judgments that usually only result in tiresome intellectualizations.

The use of very large matrices of words, even if practical, would not protect us from the dangers of omission or over- or underrepresentation of concepts, words, or semantic dimensions. Such mistakes are particularly likely and consequential in cross-cultural research. If, following the American conceptualization of education, we use the words "school," "learning," and "intelligence" to study this domain in Korean, we are likely to miss characteristically Korean components of education such as moral character, behavioral norms, and the teacher—student relationship. Only by including words representative of these dimensions will we be able to identify these components.

This problem, which calls for the use of culturally representative word samples, is coupled with the various technical limitations of factor analysis, such as the commonly low percentage of variance accounted for and the difficulties in the identification of a sufficient number of factors. In this relational strategy, then, the assessment of single word meanings is seriously limited by the difficulties in obtaining representative samples of semantic domains and the technical problems of processing and factor analyzing large word samples.

Generally, we may conclude that in the analysis of psychological meaning, the identification of the main components and the assessment of their dominance constitute critical key problems. The two major research strategies explored offer different, partially complementary approaches. The direct analysis of semantic components focuses on the meanings of single words, whereas the analysis of semantic relations relies on word samples and works through the identification of semantic dimensions.

As each of these approaches has its advantages and limitations, a method that can work at both levels is desirable. Such a method would combine the inferential nature of the relational strategy of assessment with the simplicity of the direct method and its potential to focus on single words. Such a combination seems to be possible by relying on a strategy that exploits word associations as a source of information about psychological meaning.

ASSOCIATIONS AND MEANING

The notion of association has had a long and honorable history in psychology. That history has been traced many times, and in recent years three books (Cramer, 1668; Creelman, 1966; Deese, 1965) have been devoted in whole or part to an exposition of that history. We need not review that history but only note that, for our purposes, it has two chief components. One is the notion of association as process and the other is the study of associations by eliciting them from human beings. Until very recently, it has simply been taken for granted that the idea of association-as-process, as it has come down to us from Aristotle, is meant somehow to account for or explain the associations we can elicit from people. More recently, however, we have begun to realize that free associations and other derivatives of the association method in experimentation and clinical practice can be viewed as short-hand expressions of the kinds of things that can be expressed by such linguistic entities as propositions, sentences, and, indeed, entire discourses (Clark, 1970; Deese & Hamilton, 1974). In short, we no longer need to argue that the use of the association method in experimentation automatically implies a faith in what historically are processes of association — contiguity and frequency. Rather, associations are simply a remarkably easy and efficient way of determining the contents of human minds without having those contents expressed in the full discursive structure of language. In fact, there is good reason for believing, as Galton (1880) pointed out at the very beginning of the empirical investigations of associations, and as Freud (1924) realized early, that the association method reveals the content of minds in a way that propositional language does not. We can and do reveal ourselves in associations in ways that we might find difficult to do if we were required to spell out the full propositions behind our associations. The use of the free-association method in psychoanalysis is built upon a recognition of the depths of mind that free associations tap.

Association-as-Process

Although we may be excused from reviewing the history of the various notions of association-as-process, a word of comment on one aspect of that history and its relation to contemporary semantic theory is in order. As Aarsleff (1970) now reminds us, the kind of semantic feature theory generally made popular by Katz and Fodor (1963) has its parallel if not its origin in Locke's notion of the development of complex ideas through the association of simple ideas. Locke's and Hume's notions of mental mechanics — a combination of elements that retained their original qualities — is much closer to contemporary semantic feature theory than the mental chemistry of Hartley and James and John Stuart Mill, in which the elements compounded form a new unit more or less different from the sum of the components. Suffice it to say once again, we may, for our purposes, ignore the difference between Locke and Hume on the one hand and Hartley and James and John Stuart Mill on the other by regarding the associative method as revealing the content of mental representation or subjective meaning, as that content can be expressed in an indefinitely large number of propositions. In much the same way, the use of the associative method does not commit us to one or another of the current views as to the nature of semantic structure.

While we may thus safely dismiss the history of association-as-process, an account of the various associative methods as they have been developed in the past century is germane to our purpose. There is a direct continuity between these earlier uses of the associative methods and the uses to which they have been put in the cross-cultural investigations reported in this book.

Though Galton's (1880) experiments are the earliest, Wundt's (1883) association experiments served as the model influential not only for experimental psychologists but for such psychiatrists as Bleuler, Jung, and, to a lesser extent, even Freud. At the turn of the century, associations were envisioned as providing sensitive analytic instruments of diagnostic value. Founders of the leading psychoanalytic schools shared the view that associations could be used effectively in the identification of emotion-laden experiences and complexes that were hidden causes of neuroses with roots in the subconscious.

Association in the Psychoanalytic Method

As is well known, Freud's primary use of associations was in dream analysis. As the patients relaxed on the couch or in an easy chair, they were asked to tell what came to mind in connection with a selected word, image, or idea. The words Freud used to elicit free associations came from the patients' dreams. The patients were told not to withhold any response, but say everything that came into their mind. The patients, concentrating on the word, might produce one or more associations, which the analyst would record. Freud (1924) characterized this process as a "search after meaning" or "latent content." He pointed out that searching for meaning through direct questions was of little use for several reasons. For one thing, elements of latent content often appeared to be trivial, embarrassing, or shameful. Freud illustrated by numerous examples that associations could provide insights that could not have been obtained by direct questions. Despite their appearance of being ad hoc and accidental, Freud observed, associations were definite reactions determined by the specific dispositions of the responding person — "inner attitudes" that reflected "complexes" with strong emotional foundation.

Freud's interest in associations was narrowly focused on the identification of "latent content," a strong, internal, emotional foundation resulting from suppressed experiences affecting the ego. This focus followed from his position that the cure of neuroses requires the identification of their hidden causes. He ignored those categories of associations in which he saw no therapeutic relevance.

In Freud's interpretation, associations derive from meaning as an internal, psychological content. External events produce associations only through their internal representation. The value of the association is in its potential to inform on internal processes. Among these, affects — psychodynamic forces and conflicts — receive primary attention, whereas intellect and purely cognitive variables are assigned merely secondary roles.

The method Freud adopted in the elicitation of associations is consistent with his rationale and deserves particular attention in the present context. The patients were encouraged to give as many responses as they could. Although since Wundt it had been customary to ask for a single response to each stimulus, Freud employed what has later been called "the method of continuous association." Furthermore, it was customary to urge patients to give an immediate response, but Freud merely asked them to respond spontaneously without selectivity. One reason for this was the important role Freud assigned to the superego — its resistance, its censorship of responses. Not interpreting associations in the framework of a stimulus—response paradigm, he saw no information value in reaction time. Other clinical approaches show various degrees of similarity to Freud's method. Particularly in America, such uses have been influenced by the stimulus—response paradigm of experimentalists.

Associative Meaning

Largely through the influence of Ebbinghaus (1885), the methods used to study association in the laboratory became antithetical to the study of meaning. Ebbinghaus's goal of studying the association process free from that influence of previously learned meaning became an obsession with laboratory investigators, and any relevance laboratory experiments may have had for the investigation of meaning all but disappears from Ebbinghaus until the development of the famous Minnesota norms (Russell & Jenkins, 1954). After these norms became available, there quickly developed a sense of the relevance of associations for meaning, and something closer to the analysis suggested by Freud rather than classical association theory became the guiding principle of investigations.

We now need to turn to a brief account of the various procedures in the investigation of meaningful associations. Typically, such investigations use single words as the stimulus objects, although that is by no means a necessity. Pictures, odors, entire sentences, and propositions, among other things, have been used as stimuli. Various tasks or sets can be given to the experimental subjects. Two of the most important aspects of the tasks are labeled free and controlled. In free association, subjects are instructed to respond with any word or idea that occurs to them on the presentation of the stimulus. In controlled association, a selected category of responses is called for. For example, subjects may be required to respond with opposites or with superordinates.

Further, the tasks or instructions may call for discrete or continued associations. Discrete association requires but a single response. Continued association calls for more than one response, sometimes a specific number and sometimes simply as many as the subject can give within a limited time. Another variation calls for continuous association, a method closer to the probing technique of the psychoanalyst. For example, beginning with the stimulus *table,* the successive responses might be *chair, sit, stand, firm, concrete, building,* etc.

The discrete free-association task is perhaps the most widely used because it is ideally suited to the prevailing stimulus–response paradigm and because it eliminates the influence of previous responses. At the same time, it presents some problems for the evaluation of responses to a given stimulus. If we are to get any idea of the range and distribution of responses elicited by a single stimulus, we must combine in *response norms* the single associations of a large number of individuals. Such a procedure eliminates idiosyncratic meanings in order to achieve a kind of statistical picture of reactions of a particular group of individuals.

Categorizing Associations

Other approaches focus on qualitative rather than quantitative aspects of associations and use various types of categorization. Since Galton's (1880) first association experiments, a constantly recurring idea has been making sense out of associations by assigning them to categories. Galton used such categories as visual and other images, histrionic representations (acting out events or attitudes), and purely verbal associations (names, quotations). Jung's (1919) categories were coordination, sub- and supraordination, contrast, predicate expressing a personal judgment, simple predicate, relation of the verb to subject or complement, designation of time, definition, coexistence, identity, matter–speech combination, composition of words, completion of words, Klang associations, and defective reactions. Woodworth and Schlosberg (1954) used definitions, synonyms, supraordinates, completion and predication, coordinates and contrasts, and valuations and personal associations.

Some of the many category systems developed capitalize on dimensions relevant to clinical analysis; others utilize primarily linguistic or grammatical categories. The choice depends on the frame of reference of the investigator. Since each investigator generates categories according to his or her own interest, the system thus becomes an instrument for projecting orientations of the investigator rather than reflecting the natural aspects of the association process. In these various systems, the same response may obtain different interpretations.

The response *girl*[1] elicited by the stimulus *boy* would be a "purely verbal" reaction, a "name" according to Galton. It might be a "coordinate" or "coexistence" reaction to Jung and a "coordinate" or a "contrast" to Woodworth and Schlosberg. And it could be an "opposite," a "partial synonym," a "paradigmatic response," or something else in terms of other category systems.

Associations as Statements

Such confusions reveal a fundamental fact about associations, namely, that they are not complete in themselves. They are truncated ways of saying something that never gets fully articulated and that, when articulated, must reveal only partially what was meant. Thus, a particular person may be saying something like, "boy is the opposite of girl," when he responds *boy* to *girl*, or may be saying something more complicated, such as "boys and girls are both members of the class, human beings." There is no way to tell. All we know is that the concepts *boy* and *girl* are intimately related because so many people give them as associates to one another, particularly in our culture. That is the great strength of associative data. When we are free to pursue the context of an individual association, as in psychoanalysis, associative data can reveal some very particular reason why someone wants to say X when stimulated by Y. Deese and Hamilton (1974) pointed out that there are strong reasons for believing that the associative response is a kind of statement about the stimulus. That is, the experimental subject or the psychoanalytic patient produces something about which the stimulus is about. That is what makes associations such powerful probes of mental content. Citizens of Colombia, who are likely to say *polite* to *educated* (p. 35), are telling us something about their attitudes towards education — perhaps that only educated people are polite. In so doing, they incidentally reveal a great deal about their culture that they might otherwise have been unable to express.

Parameters of Associations

Several association-based measures provide data on such parameters of meaning and meaningfulness and similarity. Noble's (1952) measure of "meaningfulness" relies on the number of associations to a particular stimulus word in a continued-association task with a 60-second time limit. Experiments show (Noble, 1952; Terwilliger, 1964; Underwood, 1959) that it is a valid measure of the richness of meaning. This measure does not reveal what meaning is or what the components of the meaning reaction are, but it does show how inclusive, how rich the mean-

---

[1]All associative responses, stimuli, and concepts inferred from distributions of associations will be in italics.

ing reaction is, how meaningful the word is to a particular person or group. This parameter of meaning becomes manifest only in continued-association tasks. It has no opportunity to emerge from discrete tasks and is apparently contaminated by other factors in continuous ones (Wispé, 1954).

A second natural parameter of meaning is similarity. Although the total distribution in continued association reveals the richness of meaning to a particular individual, it does not tell us anything of how the meaningful reaction to that particular stimulus is related to the reaction to other stimuli. The shared elements of two responsive distributions, obtained from either discrete or continued association, can tell us something quantitatively about the psychological meaning shared by two stimuli. Given the importance of similarity in meaning, it is not surprising that there have been a large number of indices designed to take the measure of such a relation. Some of the best known are mutual frequency (Cofer, 1957), mutual relatedness (Bousfield, Whitmarsh, & Berkowitz, 1960), commonality or intersection (Deese, 1965), relatedness (Garskof & Houston, 1963), cohesiveness (Pollio, 1964), and conditional probabilities (Mackenzie, 1972). These indices all have in common the use of the shared associations of two response distributions to index how similar two stimuli are in meaning. With the exception of Garskof and Houston's relatedness coefficient, they all apply to discrete associative tasks, a fact that limits their applicability to groups.

In simple terms, two stimuli may be said to have the same associative meaning when the distributions of their associations are identical, and they may be said to share meaning to the extent that these distributions agree (Deese, 1965). The question is: Is such a conclusion compelling only to someone who assumes, as Deese does, that the distribution of verbal associations describes the meaning reaction? On procedural considerations alone, the conclusion is plausible, but there are data that establish the convergent validity of the view that such distributions reflect underlying similarities and perhaps structural relations in meaning. Factor analysis of matrices of intersection or overlap measures produces factors that inform on components of meaning characteristic of the domains under investigation. Thus, for instance, when Deese (1963) factor analyzed a matrix of intersection coefficients on a sample of words involving *butterfly* and its most frequent associates, he obtained six factors including animate (*bees, flies*), non-animate (*sky, spring*), and flying (*bird, wing*). Laffal and Feldman (1962) obtained closely similar results on an analogous sample of words representing associates to *butterfly*. Furthermore, Deese (1965) has been able to show that the structures emerging from underlying indices of similarity are correlated with the patterns people employ when they must learn by rote arbitrary connections between the words in the structures. The implication is that people actually use such structures when learning by rote, an implication widely accepted today, and that such meaningful structures may be well described by patterns in associations. Finally, Henley (1969) was able to show that multidimensional scaling of judgments of similarity produced very much the same kinds of patterns as the factor analysis of associative data.

USING ASSOCIATIONS TO STUDY SUBJECTIVE CULTURE

With this much background we can turn to the details of the relation between associations and psychological or subjective meaning. Our purpose is to provide a framework upon which we can hang the analysis of cross-cultural data that comprises the majority of this book.

Associations and Propositions

One of the most important conceptual changes that has recently happened in cognitive psychology is the assimilation of the associative relationship to linguistic structures generally. Anderson and Bower (1973), in their book *Human Associative Memory*, used association to refer to the relations among the elements or nodes in any structure. Almost any account of mental processes from classical associationism through stimulus–response theory to theories of linguistic processing based upon transformation grammars as well as theories of artificial intelligence can be so described. Anderson and Bower, to the extent that they would be concerned, would describe the associations found in experiments on free association as being truncated versions of propositional structures in much the same way that they regard the associative structures in their earlier program concerned with paired-associate learning to be encompassed by the more general structure of HAM.

To say that free associations express propositions is simply to give them the character of the most general class of linguistic relations. It enables us to abolish a distinction between meaningless and meaningful associations, for they all may be represented in some abstract structure, such as HAM, in the same way. Meaningfulness is reflected in the richness or number of propositions that can be generated about a particular concept. That, in turn, provides us with a measure of the subjective meaningfulness of any particular concept. Noble (1952) was quite right to use rate of associations as a kind of rough index of the meaningfulness of a word. We may simply regard his *m* as a kind of measure of the rate at which people of a certain educational and cultural background can generate propositions about a particular word. The propositions, of course, are only incompletely realized by associations and, as we shall point out repeatedly, the incompleteness of associations is the price we pay for their spontaneous character and ability to reveal subjective meaning.

Consider the associations of the word *hammer. Nail, tool, saw, hit, sickle,* and *pound* are all common responses given by various groups of American subjects to *hammer*. We may take these all as telling us something about what these subjects know, believe, and feel about the concept *hammer*. One uses a *hammer* to *hit nails.* A *hammer,* like a *saw,* is a *tool.* The *hammer* and *sickle* is a political symbol. One *pounds* with a *hammer,* and so on. Viewed in this way, it is easy to account for these associations out of our own experience. But suppose someone says *swim* to *hammer.* We cannot so easily find a propositional structure here. Perhaps it is the case that our subject is a schizophrenic. Or, perhaps he knows something that we do not know. The point is that such a response is not different in principle, only more difficult for us to account for from a limited cultural perspective. If we were to collect a large number of associations to *hammer* from the person who gave *swim,* we could learn something about him and about the cultural matrix in which he is embedded. Indeed, that is the major point of this book.

Suppose someone who speaks Chinese, for example, but who knows no English says *nail to hammer.* What are we to conclude? If we know for sure that he knows no English, we must regard this as revealing some proposition such as "*Nail* is a sound I have heard English speakers say after the word *hammer.*" A person who knows no Latin might well give *liberabit* to *Veritas* because *liberabit* completes the well-known Latin phrase *veritas vos liberabit* that he might have heard often expressed. The point is that one cannot tell the extent of the meaningfulness of a particular association without some further context. As we have indicated, a particularly useful way to establish that context is to obtain additional associations to the same term, something that can lead to the use of rate of association as an index of meaningfulness. Sometimes the context to a particular association must be provided by other information, e.g., that the person giving the association is a schizophrenic or does not speak English.

Viewing associations as propositional is simply another way of saying that they are linguistic; however, a word of caution must be expressed. Propositions are ordinarily embedded in discourse, and, as much of contemporary linguistic theory informs us, the structure of discourse depends upon the demands of communication. Associations are free from the intent to communicate some particular, organized discourse. They are simply the expression of thought. That is what provides their unique character and usefulness. It is apparently easier, as the earliest investigators of free association discovered, to express one's thoughts when the relations among words are free from the demands of syntax and morphology.

Stimuli in the Control of Propositions

There is another matter of paramount importance that must be mentioned at this point. We have already pointed out that there is a procedural difference between discrete and continued association on the one hand and continuous association on the other. Continuous association has many, although not all, of the properties of discourse. Unlike discourse, it is not usually dominated by some topic about which statements are made in an organized way. Rather, topics change, come and go. But at least there is a kind of narrative property. For discrete and continued association, on the other hand, all continuity is provided from the outside. Part of each statement or proposition is provided by investigators in the form of the free-associational stimulus. Thus, the investigators are able to control what particular things their respondents think about. Thus, to say that associations can be expressed as ordinary statements or propositions is not to say that they are the same as statements in ordinary discourse. Associations have a character of spontaneity that is a result of their freedom from an overall plan of discourse. This spontaneity permits them to reveal aspects of subjective meaning that could not be revealed if respondents had to spell out the associations obtained.

Focusing on Meaning

The above analysis of the process of association generally supports the contention that tasks and measures originally designed in the context of a stimulus—response conceptualization create and perpetuate strong predispositions to focus on uninterpretable single responses and disregard the larger structures. As long, then, as the style of experimentation is heavily influenced by this verbal-habit orientation and as long as single-response tasks and measures focused on "response strength" dominate the field of experimentation, strong disposition is likely to persist that will hamper investigators in taking advantage of the information offered by the distribution of verbal associations.

The rationale of the meaning-mediated view of verbal association accordingly favors the use of continued association tasks over discrete ones. Furthermore, it favors the use of measures that focus upon the total distributions of associations and examine their basic characteristics. Fundamentally, the central issue in association is not the single connection but rather the meaning of the stimulus embedded in a matrix of knowledge.

The Characterization of Cultures

Systems of knowledge are reflected in cultures, and it is to an understanding of cultures and cultural differences that our use of the associative method is primarily addressed. The study of culture is traditionally the domain of anthropologists. Faced with the diversity of human behavior across cultures, these investigators have searched for higher order concepts that can provide for an objective, scientific study of the varieties of human behavior and their organization. The empirical orientation of anthropology has resulted in a focus upon the individual and the personality of cultures. Such largely intuitive concepts as "national genius" have gradually and systematically been replaced by more empirically based concepts such as "modal personality." Descriptive accounts are increasingly being complemented by tests and measurements.

At an earlier stage, it was common to borrow personality concepts from philosophers like Dilthey and Spranger or from the leaders of the various psycho-analytic schools. For example, Ruth Benedict's concept of "configurational personality" relies on variety of diverse personality types. A related concept, "national character," became popular during and after World War II and is represented by such studies as Mead's (1942) investigation of American character, Gorer and Rickman's (1949) and Bauer, Inkeles, and Kluckhohn's (1956) study of the Russian character, and Benedict's (1946) investigation of the Japanese character. The popularity of national-character studies may be partially explained by the fact that, although frequently intuitive in nature and lacking in scientific rigor, they managed to avoid the frustrating theoretical and methodological problems characteristic of the concept and measurement of personality. The concept of modal personality constitutes a further stage of development. In its genesis, modal personality was viewed as a product of "organismic tendencies" reinforced by the specific experiences, conditions, and systems of rewards characteristic of a particular cultural environment.

As Inkeles and Levinson (1954) observed, although the central concept of these various approaches appears to be personality, most anthropological studies focus on institutions as the mold of personality or on myths and folktales as products of personality rather than on personality as an actual psychological structure. This collective focus shows that in speaking of personality, anthropologists have in mind not a particular person, but a prototype by which groups can be characterized. It is preoccupied with common characteristics and the foundation of these characteristics in collective practices and social institutions. Furthermore, some of these approaches fail to describe cultures in their own terms, but instead apply high level abstractions from Western culture.

Another approach is represented by ethnolinguistics. One important source of interest behind ethnolinguistics can be traced back to the assumption that language exerts strong influences on thought processes and world view. This partially explains why investigations in this field frequently show a strong linguistic orientation, some focusing on classification systems, such as Hallowell's (1949) study of the Ojibwa tribe, and some on terminology, such as the componential analysis introduced by Lounsbury (1956) and Goodenough (1956, 1965).

Componential analysis uses what we called earlier a logical–linguistic approach.Its utility is largely confined to certain semantic domains, such as kinship taxonomies, that can be analyzed in terms of such attributes as male vs. female or consanguineal vs. lateral. Burling (1964) has raised some doubts about the adequacy of such analyses. Often the intent is to describe psychological meaning, but what they do is provide a structure that can account for certain kinds of usage. Indeed, Romney and D'Andrade (1964) have demonstrated through multidimensional scaling based upon triadic judgments, that of three different analyses of English kinship terms, only one accorded with the structure derived from the similarity analysis.

In contrast with the logically oriented linguistic analysis, other methods focus on subjectively perceived similarity relations. Thus, Metzger and Williams (1966), Conklin (1964), and D'Andrade, Quinn, Nerlove, and Romney (1972) have used a "frame elicitation" technique to identify culturally salient attributes and to reconstruct culturally characteristic similarity relationships. Similarity judgment tasks and sentence-frame methods are sensitive techniques now being used by numerous anthropologists for the analysis and mapping of cognitive organization. There is a close relationship between these methods and those used by psychologists who aim to reconstruct cognitive organization and culture through the study of psychological meaning (see Deese, 1976).

Among ethnolinguists, Wallace (1956) has made particularly explicit the idea of a cognitive map as a representational system in his concept of "mazeways." For Wallace, the mazeway constitutes all the mental images a person uses. These images are thought to consist of a large number of beliefs or propositions. Wallace compared the mazeway to a gigantic map that represents goals and pitfalls, the self and other objects, and plans and techniques that may be used to attain goals. The idea of subjective representation of the universe is also central to Whorf's (1956) "thought world," which he describes as a "microcosm that each man carries about within himself, by which he measures and understands what he can of the macrocosm" (p. 147). Brown (1964) observed. "For ethnoscience the mind seems to be a categorical grid imposed on reality, rendering some things equivalent and others nonequivalent. Since the cells of the grid are usually named, the design of the grid should be discoverable from inquiries about the meanings of words" (p. 251).

Among psychologists, Osgood (1964) and Triandis and his colleagues (Triandis, 1964; Triandis, Vassiliou, & Nassiakou, 1968), have been concerned in a very similar way with "subjective culture." Triandis and Vassiliou (1967) also used the metaphor of a map. The map, in this case, is the way in which individuals conceive of their environment. He argued that such maps, which will differ from culture to culture, constitute the basis for different kinds of behavior in different cultures.

Even without invoking the work of Dorothy Lee or the whole French school of structuralism, it is amply apparent that all of the sciences concerned with the psychological nature of man have found it necessary to suppose that human beings have some way of representing nature, themselves, and indeed the world in subjective terms. For our own part, we prefer to describe this subjective world as the subjective representational system. We shall argue, in the course of this book, that free associations provide a remarkably fruitful, perhaps best way of obtaining some notion about what that system is like. The system, we hasten to add, is not a linguistic one. It may be reflected in images, or indeed in any activity that reflects knowledge, beliefs, attitudes, or affectivity. Through the system, the world is translated into an internalized subjective representation. This representation must reflect which aspects of the world receive representation, how much attention they receive, and what position they occupy in a hierarchy of subjective priorities or importance. Although aspects of it remain stable over long periods of time, it is dynamic and depends upon motives and needs.

Using Associations to Characterize Cultures

Before introducing the assumptions we make in order to connect associations with this subjective representation, perhaps an example will help show, in an intuitive way, how associations do inform us about the subjective world. Suppose we ask two individuals, one a Black American and the other a White American, to give as many associations to the word *freedom* in one minute as they can. The Black person gives *free, slave, Blacks, love, peace, good, jail, Whites, speech*. The White individual gives *free, speech, life, U.S., love, liberty, religion*, and *flag*. Notice, by the way, if we had used the method of discrete association, we would not have learned how these two individuals differ, for both gave *free* as the first response.

What do these reactions tell us? The response *slavery* tells us that, for the Black respondent, *slavery* is still an active component of his contemporary meaning of *freedom*. It is important to him in a way that it is not to the White person that *freedom* contrasts with *slavery*. His response *Blacks* shows that he thinks of *freedom* as something that bears directly on *Black* existence.

As we shall point out shortly, the order in which associations is given is important. In general, the earlier the response, the more salient the component of meaning revealed by the response. By this notion, for the Black person, that component revealed by the response *slavery* is more salient in the subjective representation of *freedom* than is *jail*. By the same token, *free speech* is evidently more salient in the conception of *freedom* for the White individual than for the Black.

Responses that are related by lexical criteria or related to the stimulus in much the same way may be combined to reveal broader concerns within the subjective representation. For example, the Black person's responses of *jail* and *slavery* suggest a central concern for lack of freedom. When we combine various responses we discover that *freedom* for the Black person has strong racial concerns, whereas for the White person it has patriotic implications.

The example, of course, is an artificial one but is based upon the data obtained from two large samples of Black and White individuals (Szalay, Bryson, & West, 1973), described later in this book. It serves to illustrate that free associations inform us about subjective culture. The bits of information obtained from examining distributions of associations to one word and comparing them with distributions to other words provide us with a detailed picture of some domain of subjective meaning. We can see, for example, that the notion of *freedom* for Blacks is inseparable from questions of race.

Associations make meaningful statements. That they do not make use of the syntax and other grammatical features of ordinary statements does not disqualify them from being meaningful. Their simplicity and immediacy makes them, however, much closer to the stable, significant aspects of the subjective representation of the world than an equivalent set of fully articulated sentences about the stimuli. We shall return to this point in a later chapter.

DOMINANCE, AFFINITY, AND AFFECTIVITY

Our subjective representations of the world have certain universal characteristics. Some domains are more central to our lives than are others. Family and familial relations may be fundamental to a particular culture and, thus, occupy a most prominent role in the subjective representations of persons in that culture. Within domains, certain particular concepts may be more important than others. Thus, the notion of *ancestor* is more important to the typical Korean than to the typical American. Furthermore, our subjective world is organized. Certain concepts form clusters that are related in meaning. Finally, affectivity suffuses the subjective world. These three aspects of the subjective representational system provide a kind of organization around which we can portray important relations in subjective meaning. We have labeled these three aspects dominance, affinity, and affectivity.

The notion of dominance simply recognizes the fact that within the totality of subjective meaning, certain concepts are more important or central than are others. It is similar to notions like salience (Miller, 1967), centrality (Harvey, Hunt, & Schroeder, 1961; Rokeach, 1960), and ordinal hierarchy (Kelly, 1963).

Affinity recognizes the fact that subjective meaning is organized. Certain concepts are more closely related to one another than are other concepts. Such subjective organization is universally recognized by students of the subjective lexicon, and there have been many attempts to characterize it and capture it in various measures of relation (see Fillenbaum & Rapoport, 1971). In Chapter 2 we propose a way of capturing, through a kind of statistical index, such relations in association. Although we make use of such an index to specify the magnitude of affinal relations in a rough way, we recognize that the relations themselves are qualitatively different from one another and must be interpreted in various ways.

Affectivity simply recognizes the fact that we evaluate most things positively or negatively, and, even for those concepts we may not evaluate, we always have the potential for so doing. Affectivity is a fundamental component of attitudes and most beliefs as well, so it is a central part of our analysis of subjective meaning and culture.

The viewpoint implicit in these assumptions has developed from experience in the analysis of word-association data obtained in a wide variety of research settings over the past 15 years. The first author, in particular, has collected data from American, Korean, Hispanic, and Arabic sources and has used these data to reconstruct the representational system characteristic of a particular social or cultural group. This is a sizable, although not unmanageable, task. An analysis of the representational system characteristic of a culture can be effectively performed by relying on 150 to 200 stimuli, representing themes systematically selected to reflect dominant cultural domains. Rather than presenting the results in terms of the analysis of specific cultural features, the following chapters focus primarily on the analytic procedures involved in examining the utility of word associations for studying subjective culture.

A final point: Associations are not subjective meaning, nor are the statements realizable from them subjective meaning. Rather, subjective meaning is a domain of its own, some of the structural properties of which may be discovered by considering associations and the propositions implied by those associations. Human thought processes are not to be found in language or in images or in any particular manifestation. The content of our mental representations is transformed into these things, and we regard associations as but one of the outcomes of mental representation. They are closer to those representations than is ordinary language for they are not filtered by the need to communicate intention, and their linguistic simplicity makes them more immediate and spontaneous than is ordinary language.

2 The Associative Method Applied

In the previous chapter we argued that associations were capable of yielding significant information about the attitudes, beliefs, and cognitive structures of individuals and social and cultural groups. In this chapter we outline a method for gathering associative data for purposes of obtaining such information. Further, we present a method for treating associative data that is particularly useful in portraying social and group differences. In general, we have called our technique *the method of associative group analysis.*

ASSOCIATIVE GROUP ANALYSIS

First of all, a method of continued association provides the data-gathering technique. We prefer this method to that of discrete association both because of the larger amount of information it provides for each individual tested and because it allows for a richer analysis of the data from smaller samples. In the following pages we outline general methods; specific information about sample sizes, reliability procedures, etc., follows in the chapters devoted to particular results.

Method of Testing

Characteristically, testing is in groups with written responses. Working without time pressure with a written form of the associative test tends to promote meaningful responses and reduces the frequency of klang associates. If people are asked to respond immediately to an orally presented word, there is a good chance that phonemic or phonetic properties will play a greater role in producing responses than if time pressure did not exist. Siipola, Walker, & Colb (1955) observed: "when time pressure is relaxed, the associative process undergoes a fundamental change in character" (p. 445). Under time pressure, the associations are "stimulus bound (verbal), impersonal, and mechanical;" without it, the association process becomes "truly free" and "rich in personal meaning" (p. 445).

Furthermore, the written form of an associative test provides for relatively greater neutrality and impersonal atmosphere than does an oral test. It minimizes the possibility that the subjects will respond not merely to the stimulus but to the test administrator as well. The impersonal character of the test situation is emphasized by the use of group sessions. Finally, subjects are not identified by name. Anonymity reduces any tendency subjects may have to edit their responses.

On occasion, these general conditions may be altered. For example, when testing illiterates, respones are usually tape recorded. When the associative testing is carried out in the context of interviews, of course, testing is individual and oral.

Samples

Experience shows that a sample of between 50 and 100 individuals will provide stable data. Representativeness of the samples, as in attitude and survey research, is a problem. In general, we have preferred to use matched samples of particular groups rather than to attempt representative sampling on some very general (e.g., national) level. We have tended to focus on specific comparisons rather than very general ones. For example, we have compared Black and White policemen from the 3rd precinct of Washington, D.C., and Puerto Rican students and Black students matched by field of study at Columbia University.

Relevance of Themes

Another important problem related to the question of sampling and comparison is that of the relevance of themes. It is necessary to identify ahead of time themes that are significant to a particular group. If one is interested in a comparison, it often turns out that themes relevant to one group are not relevant to another. People do not always think about such broad domains as education, for example, in the same terms. To solve this problem, a test administered by two groups for comparative purposes should always contain items relevant to the themes for both groups, even if it means that the responses to some of the items will not be useful for one or another of the groups.

The particular items that are selected for a given test depend, of course, upon the scope and nature of the inquiry. Narrow and clearly focused applications, such as the assessment of racial images, call for a relatively few specific stimuli (e.g., *Black, White*) that can be easily identified on the basis of objectives of the research. Broader applications, such as the determination of a "subjective culture" or the measurement of "psychocultural distance" between two groups, require substantially more stimulus items, sometimes systematically selected through the use of as many as three consecutive associative tasks.

The number of themes used in the representation of some domain will, of course, vary. For example, a few words such as *mother, father, home,* and *security* may serve to represent the domain *family* in a study that is wide in scope and embraces several domains. On the other hand, if the major research interest is in the domain *family*, it will be desirable to use more themes on roles (*child, son, sister, relatives*), relevant roles (*love, friendship, partnership*), or values (*cohesion, loyalty*).

The number of words is a less delicate problem, however, than is the criterion that the themes used should be representative of the domains. This requirement may be explained by an example. The themes previously mentioned in the context of *family* generally appear as common sense to the average American. However, for Koreans, some of them, such as *friendship* and *partnership*, may appear entirely out of place in the representation of the *family* domain, just as *ancestors, filial duty,* and *solidarity* — themes relevant to *family* for Koreans — would not be among the themes an American would think of in this connection.

The way to solve this problem is to pretest, using the domains themselves as the stimuli. The associations commonly given to the names of the domains will provide the themes appropriate to the particular group tested. Combining such responses from several groups will then provide a master list representative for all groups involved.

TESTING THE SUBJECTS

Because the method outlined below requires 1 minute of associations to each stimulus word, an hour's testing, allowing time for instructions, usually will provide data on 40 or so stimulus words.

A test session usually begins with the test administrator explaining that the test is a group test and not a measure of individual performance. Those being tested are told that the administrator is not interested in names or personal information, but in order to categorize the results properly, the administrator will ask the subjects to fill in a short questionnaire containing such information as sex and age.

Instructions

The standard instructions for testing are as follows:

This experiment is part of a study in verbal behavior, and this particular task involves word associations.

These are group experiments, and your responses will not be evaluated individually but collectively for your group. Your responses are completely anonymous, and you are free to give your associations concerning any subject. There are no bad or wrong answers, so do not select your responses but put them down spontaneously in the order that they occur to you.

The task is easy and simple. You will find a word printed on each slip of paper. Reading this stimulus word will make you think of other asso-

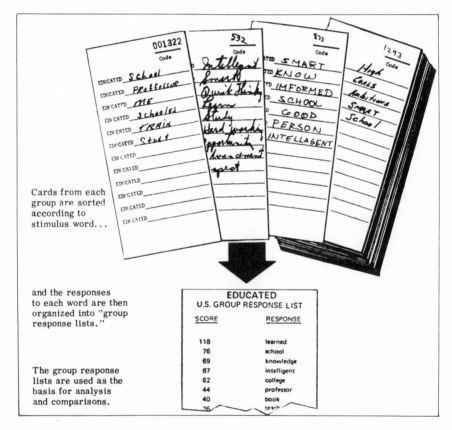

FIG. 2.1.   Some sample test sheets and an indication of how data are gathered.

ciated words (objects, ideas, issues, etc.). You are asked to write as many separate responses as you can think of in the time allotted. Try to think of one-word responses and avoid long phrases or sentences.

It is important that in giving your responses you always take the given stimulus word into consideration. For example, if the stimulus word was *table* and your answer was *writing*, in giving the subsequent responses you must refer back to *table* and avoid "chain" responses (*writing, pen, ink, blue, ocean, sail*, etc.).

Please work without hurrying, but do your best to give us as many answers as possible. One minute will be given for each word. At the end of each minute I will ask you to go on the next word. Do not work longer than one minute on any word and do not read ahead or return to others later.

Subjects, of course, always receive instructions in their native language. Each test sheet contains one stimulus word repeated as many times as necessary, with a blank space following each repetition. The sheets themselves are randomly assembled. Figure 2.1 shows a sample of test sheets for the word *educated* with responses obtained from American subjects.

Translation of Stimuli and Responses

There is, of course, a problem of translation. Stimuli must be translated into foreign languages and foreign responses translated into English. The translation of the standard stimuli from English into another language is a special problem, since these determine the nature of the data one receives. However, it should be emphasized that an associative group analysis does not depend upon the assumption that the stimulus words are always exact translations. Such an assumption would be unrealistic for cross-cultural research (Kluckhohn, 1954). Beyond simple disparities, the researcher faces untranslatable terms such as *l'espirit, Weltanschauung, simpático.*

Because semantic disparities between words of culturally distinct languages are more the rule than the exception, the research strategy must focus on equivalents, that is, stimuli that may not mean exactly the same but that allow the tapping of English and foreign response repertoires at comparable places in the two representational systems. Where exact translations are lacking, selections are made of words closest in meaning – those words the native speaker would be compelled to use to communicate on the same topic. When *hungry* is translated into Korean, for example, a Korean word of exactly the same meaning may not be available. The closest word might be *baegop'un*, a word with a meaning something between "hungry" and "starving." Since Koreans ordinarily use this term to express the state resulting from lack of food, the word would be accepted as the closest available translation equivalent in Korean for the English word *hungry*. Semantic disparities should not discourage cross-cultural research on meanings. Rather, they derive from general cultural characteristics.

In the planning stage the original English stimulus word list will contain a large number of words. This list is then translated by bilinguals who are active speakers of the foreign language and also competent in English. Translations that are different are next translated into English. Where there are difficulties in finding a single unequivocal term, occasionally two foreign alternative translations may be used. In other instances, the English word is dropped from the list. By this method, a final word list is derived containing stimuli with approximate translation equivalents in both languages.

The translation of the responses is a much more extensive task, but a substantially less sensitive one, because conclusions are based on the total distribution of responses rather than on a single response. In performing the translation, a bilingual expert in each language makes all translations, and another checks his or her work. In instances of conflicting opinions, additional translations are consulted.

WEIGHTING THE RESPONSES

When persons give multiple responses to a single word, as required by the continued-associative method, there is the problem of whether to treat the earlier responses differently from the later ones. Common sense, associative theory, and the empirical literature on associations unite in supporting the view that earlier responses are somehow more central to the representational system than the later ones. The distribution of frequency against rank order of frequency in discrete association is generally steep and negatively accelerated (Horvath, 1963; Howes, 1957). It is frequently argued that the discrete method taps what is really salient in the mental processes of persons responding to the stimulus in question, and, therefore, the salience of the response in the first position is a great deal stronger than would be revealed by a frequency distribution of continued associations. Garskof and Houston (1963), in the method they offered for weighting responses in continued association, took something like the frequency distribution for discrete responses as the norm. Such a scheme is probably too drastic, for it is generally the case that at least the next few responses after the first one in the method of continued associations come with short latencies and some sense of immediacy on the part of the person producing them. Therefore, although we were willing to accept as reasonable the assumption that dominant or salient responses occurred earlier, we were not willing to weigh the responses by some exponential or other drastic weighting scheme.

An Empirical Basis for Weighting

It occurred to us that a very plausible assumption might help us establish an empirical basis for assigning weights to the order of respones. We argued that if the same persons are tested and then retested at some later date with the same words, dominant or salient responses ought to recur on the second testing more often than responses that are not dominant. If it is the case, then, that earlier responses are more dominant than later ones, the earlier responses should be more likely to recur on subsequent testing than the later responses.

To examine this notion, we investigated the stability of associations over a 1-week period. Twenty-one American college students gave 1 minute of continued associations to each of 32 stimulus words. The second column of Table 2.1 shows the total number of responses given to each position on the testing sheet. Notice, for example, that for the first line on the original testing sheet, the subjects gave a total of 629 responses. Since there were 32 stimuli and 21 subjects, this total should have been 672, so some of the subjects did not respond to some of the stimuli. Of those 629 responses, 381 were repeated irrespective of position (see Column 3). Therefore, about 61% of the responses in the first position reappeared in the subsequent test. In contrast, only 6 out of 48 responses in the eleventh position reappeared. It is clear that the earlier responses are most stable and, on the assumption given above, are therefore more dominant or central.

TABLE 2.1
Stability of Recurrence of Responses by Position on First Test

Position on the Testing Sheets on First Test	Total Number of Responses at this Position	Total Number of Identical Responses Recurring in Retest at Any Position on Second Test	Stability Expressed by Percent of Responses that Recurred	Weight for Scoring
1	629	381	61	6
2	613	292	48	5
3	599	242	40	4
4	589	199	34	3
5	528	172	32	3
6	465	140	30	3
7	359	91	25	3
8	268	55	21	2
9	187	29	16	2
10	124	14	11	1
11	48	6	13	1

TABLE 2.2
Comparison of U.S., Korean, and Colombian Samples to *Hungry*

U.S. Group			Korean Group			Colombian Group		
Responses	*RS[a]*	*RF[b]*	*Responses*	*RD*	*RF*	*Responses*	*RS*	*RF*
Food	220	44	Cooked rice	107	23	Meal	107	21
Eat	76	20	Beggar	100	22	Food	73	15
Thirsty	61	12	Food	51	13	Hunger	65	13
Starve	59	14	Poverty	46	9	Poor	59	14
Stomach	52	14	Rice	44	11	Beggar	43	12
Poor	43	12	Money	40	12	Poverty	38	11
Pains	27	6	People/Person	35	7	Money	36	10
People	18	5	Poor	28	6	Bread	35	9
Famished	18	5	Pitiful	27	7	Starving	29	5

[a]RS = response scores.

[b]RF = actual frequency.

The Weights

These results give us a method of weighting the responses at different positions. The weights we assigned are simply the percentages of recurrence rounded off to a single digit (see the fifth column of Table 2.1). This weighting scheme was used in the analysis of all subsequent data. It provides linear weights for the first four responses and a somewhat flatter series of weights for subsequent responses. Since slightly more than half of the data occur in the first four positions, it seems reasonable to change the slope between positions four and five.

Although we might have devised more elaborate schemes or used different weighting schemes for different sets of data, in the interests of simplicity and ease of recovering the original frequencies, we used the weighting scheme obtained from these data for all future analyses. Henceforth, "scores" refer to frequencies weighted by the numbers assigned in Column 5 of Table 2.1 to different positions.

Table 2.2 compares responses to the word *hungry* or its equivalent from three different samples, American, Korean, and Colombian.[1] Every time the response, *food*, occurred in the first position, it was given a score of 6, when it occurred in the second position, a score of 5, etc. The resulting scores are in the column under RS (response scores), while the actual frequencies are given under the columns labeled RF (actual frequency). In the Korean responses, *cooked rice* has a response score of 107. This could be obtained, for example, if 10 persons

---

[1]A more thorough account of these samples together with a detailed analysis of the data are given in Chapter 5.

TABLE 2.3
Group Responses to *Educated*

U.S. Group		Colombian Group	
Response	*Score*	*Response*	*Score*
Learned	118	Polite	80
School	76	College	77
Knowledge	69	Educated	72
Intelligent	67	Study, ious	70
College	62	University	43
Professor	44	Family	30
Book	40	Learned	29
Teacher	26	School	27
Wise, dom	26	Manners	25
People, person	23	Amiable	24
Smart	22	Education	20
Graduate	21	Friend, ly, ship	20
Man	21	Intelligent	19
Scholarly	21	Know	19
Respect	17	Professor	19
Schooled	17	Student	19
Well-rounded	17	Teacher	19
Erudite	15	Decent	18
Guess	14	Knowledge	18
Study	13	Social, able	18
Worldly	13	Book	16
Good	12	Fine, ness	15
Intellect	12	Parents	15
Knowledgeable	12	Father	14
Student	12	Habit	14
Scholar	11	Wise, dom	14
Degree	10	Example	12
Sophistication	10	Good	12
Teach	10	Professional	12
Work	10	Pupil	12
Bright	9	Culture	11
Interesting	9	Cultivated	11
Literate	9	Well-educated	11
Me	9	Teach	10
Money	9	Correct	9
Sage	9	Training, ed	9
Cultured	8	Gentlemanly	8
Diploma	8	Home	8
University	8	Agreeable	7
Helpful	7	Mother	7
Know	7	Understanding	6

(continued)

TABLE 2.3 *(continued)*

U.S. Group		Colombian Group	
Response	*Score*	*Response*	*Score*
Sense, common	7	Society	6
Development	6	Manner	6
Thoughtful	6	Children	6
Informative	6	Trip	5
Progress	5	Sacrifice	5
Lectures	5	Art	4
Satisfaction	5	Doctor	4
Reading, well read	5	Environment	4
Status	4	Language	3
Courses	4		942
Johnson (Pres.)	4		
Ideas, many	3		
	993		

gave it as their first response (RS = 60); 4, as their second response (RS = 20), and 9 persons, as their sixth response (RS = 27).

One more aspect of the method, idiosyncratic responses (responses given by a single individual), needs to be made explicit. Such responses are more important and meaningful when examining the personality of a single individual and the context in which he or she lives. In determining those features general to a social group or culture, however, such responses should be eliminated. Therefore, in the associative group analysis, only those responses given by two or more individuals are retained.

SOME EXAMPLES OF CROSS-CULTURAL COMPARISONS

Associations produced by members of our own culture appear to be sensible and comprehensible. They make common sense, and they do not seem to tell us much about ourselves that we do not already know. We are inclined to assume that our associations are so natural, so commonsensical that practically everybody would give the same responses as we do. Only by comparing our reactions with those of persons in other cultures do we discover how culture-bound our conception of common sense is. Table 2.3 compares response scores to the word *educated* given by American and Colombian college students. The dominant response for the American sample was *learned*, thereas the chief response for the Colombians was *polite*. Furthermore, *family* and *manners*, which did not appear in the American sample, received high scores in the Colombian sample. Even this kind of casual inspection informs us quickly and accurately about certain cultural differences. It also provides us with a starting point for a deeper cultural analysis. Why do Colombians and not Americans so closely associate education and politeness?

Another example: American college students gave *school, college, learn, book, teacher*, and *knowledge* as salient responses to education, where Slovenian students, tested in Ljubljana, Yugoslavia, gave *children, parents, school, good, kindergarten*, and *mother*. The notion of education elicited ideas about formal schooling (and generally at a later age) for the Americans, whereas for the Slovenians, ideas about the family predominated.

A final informal comparison involves Black, Spanish-speaking, and White American college students responding to the stimulus *United States*. The highest scores for Black Americans were for the concepts *country, American*, and *power*. For the White Americans, the highest scoring responses were *American, government*, and *freedom*. For the Spanish-Americans, the highest scoring responses were *power, capitalism*, and *freedom*. The lexical meaning of the concept *United States* surely does not differ for these three groups nor do the components of psychological meaning, for nearly all of the particular responses were shared by the three groups. But what clearly does differ is the salience or dominance of certain features in the psychological meaning to the term *United States*.

These comparisons suggest that simple response lists constitute a rich source of information. The score values express the salience of a concept and define the relationship of that concept to all the others given to a particular stimulus. The total response distribution is an extensive inventory that embraces all the elements of the group's understanding of the stimulus theme. These response distributions, however, have two main shortcomings: they have too many elements and include a much larger number of specific details than are needed. Furthermore, because they are organized by decreasing frequencies rather than by semantic affinities, they do not give us a clear idea of the semantic composition of global meaning. If, instead of ordering the list of decreasing score values, we group the responses together according to relevant semantic categories, the picture becomes simpler and more revealing.

Arriving at Culturally Relevant Categories

In order to provide such a picture, we must turn to a content analysis. Such a content analysis can take advantage of readily discernible categories. Some of these are simple lexical categories. For example, in the full distribution of response to *hungry*, the words *rice, meat, bread*, and *milk* all appear. These clearly belong to a category of foods. Other categories are subtle and sometimes psychological. For example, one could pull out of Table 2.3 all of the American responses having to do with certain attributes of a learned person — *scholarly, wise, knowledgeable*, etc. We have called such aggregates of related concepts *meaning components*. For the identification of the chief components of meaning, we have developed an analytic procedure. The responses obtained are placed in categories based upon their semantic content or relationship to the stimulus.

Rather than rely on our own judgment, we have used coders, who have the same cultural and educational background as the groups who gave the responses. If, for instance, U.S. and Colombian student groups are to be compared, United States and Colombian students are used as coders. Independently of each other, they receive lists of both U.S. and Colombian responses to the stimulus word. After the coders study the responses thoroughly, they group similar responses together and they group responses that have similar relations to the stimulus word. They typically use 8 to 12 response categories and assign all responses to these categories. The categories should be simple, not too abstract, and, in so far as possible, at the same level of generality. Responses that do not seem to fit any category are labeled miscellaneous. Responses that could be assigned with equal justification to two or more categories are put aside for further discussion. Because of the context provided by the stimulus word, however, this does not happen too often.

Coders frequently come up with different categories or assign responses differently. To reach agreement, coders meet together with a senior researcher to discuss the categories. The categories that are identical are accepted as final. Where there are discrepant categories, new alternative categories are possible, categories may be combined at a higher level, or complementary categories may result. If categories are discrepant, coders explain their rationales, and there is an effort to reach a compromise. If the disagreements cannot be resolved, the position that comes from the culture with the higher score on that response category will be accepted.

In general, agreement is high. One study of six coders working independently showed an average interjudge product-moment correlation coefficient across 76 categories of .70. The ultimate test, of course, comes in the validity of the results and that will be apparent in later chapters.

Category Labels

Category labels present a problem. One solution is to use the word with the highest score in the category. Because this would tip the category towards some culture-specific point of view, we frequently use the highest scoring response from both groups as category labels. Another solution is to hunt for as neutral a term as possible.

The data presented in Table 2.3 provide us with an example of categorical analysis. We can identify, in the context of the stimulus concept *educated*, a

TABLE 2.4
Category *Intelligence* and Category *Politeness*
Both Components of *Educated* for
American and Colombian Students

Category/ Response	Response Scores	
	U.S.	Colombian
Intelligence		
Intelligent	67	19
Intellect	12	—
Smart	22	—
Bright	9	—
Thoughtful	6	—
Sense, common	7	—
Ideas	3	—
Understanding	—	6
Total	126	25
Politeness		
Polite	—	80
Decent	—	18
Good	12	12
Respect	17	—
Fine, ness	—	—
Correct	—	9
Gentlemanly	—	8
Helpful	7	—
Agreeable	—	7
Amiable	—	24
Friendly	—	20
Social, able	—	18
Example	—	12
Manners	—	25
Manner	—	6
Total	36	254

category of responses characterizable as "intelligence." This category contains closely related responses that can be thought of as representing a component of the psychological meaning of *educated*.[2] Table 2.4 presents the responses to this category. Notice that there are important differences between American and Colombian students in the way in which this component is characterized. They both used the adjective *intelligent* or its equivalent, but the Colombian students

---

[2] As a matter of practical convenience, clusters of responses are usually labeled with two or more responses with a few dots after to indicate that the matter is open. The labels are, of course, tentative. They are intended to identify some component or part of the total meaning.

TABLE 2.5

Components of Psychological Meaning of the
Concept *Educated* for American and Colombian Students

	Response Scores	
Component	U.S. Students	Colombian Students
Family	—	80
Educators	81	50
Other persons	65	31
School	267	243
Knowledge	123	51
Learned	254	152
Intelligence	126	25
Politeness	36	254
Total	952	886
Miscellaneous	41	56
Total Responses	993	942

used *understanding*, a notion not at all found in the American characterization of the concept, whereas the Americans used *common sense, intellect,* and the probably untranslatable concept *smart.* Also notice that the score for this component was much higher for the Americans than for the Colombians.

The same table also compares the concept *politeness* as a component of the meaning of *educated* for these two groups. Notice here that the majority of words were not represented for the Americans and that the score for the component was much higher for the Colombians than for the United States students.

Table 2.5 presents all of the categories derived from the data in Table 2.3, together with the response scores for the American and Colombian students associated with them. The groups have in common strong categories of *school* and *learned.* They differed in their representation of *family* (totally absent among the Americans), *politeness* (emphasized by the Colombians), and *intelligence* (emphasized by the Americans). As we shall see later, the differences for the concept *educated* are characteristic of a whole constellation of differences in cultural experiences, life conditions, and philosophies between these two groups.

A convenient graphic way of representing the components presented in Table 2.5 is in what might be labeled a semantograph. Such a graphic display is presented in Fig. 2.2. It reveals at a glance that the U.S. students and the Colombian students differed both in the concepts represented in the meaning of *educated* and in the dominance of those components. The bars in such a presentation are arbitrarily arranged so far as their content is concerned, so this representation cannot be taken as a kind of map of some semantic space. Usually, it can be arranged so that the bars on the left-hand side show the components especially im-

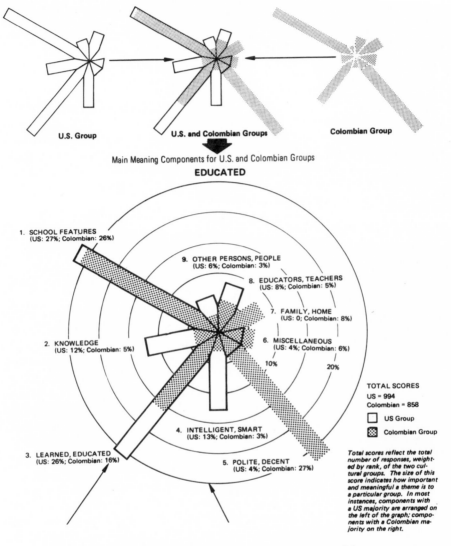

FIG. 2.2.   A graphic representation of the main components of the meaning of the concept *education* for American and Colombian students.

portant for one group, and the bars on the right represent the components
strong for the other. Such an arrangement for the Colombian and U.S. students
is approximated in Fig. 2.2.

We have, in this chapter, presented the main outline of our methods, although
certain details relevant to particular problems will be presented in later chapters.

Before going on to present the bulk of our data, however, we should say a word about the limitations of our method.

Sources of Bias

In any effort to reconstruct group meaning from the distribution of verbal associations, there are sources of biases that deserve attention. As a point of departure, it has to be fully recognized that psychological meaning determined through associations involves some degree of ambiguity and depends upon a subjective reaction that is shapeless, composite, multicomponential. As Terwilliger (1968) pointed out, some ambiguities are natural characteristics of psychological meaning. It is a common, everyday experience for us to grope for words and to be dissatisfied with the word we find for the idea we would like to express. That ambiguity is accentuated by the fact that associations are not fully formed propositions. To the extent, then, that ambiguity is intrinsic to the psychological meaning reaction, any assessment that claims to eliminate this ambiguity is likely to distort.

Our procedures introduce certain biases and distortions in other ways. There are problems endemic to the objective of identifying the components of the psychological meaning of the stimulus from the mosaic of responses actually obtained. We must rely on lexical meaning to guide us and that will surely lose some of the nuances of psychological meaning. Without knowing exactly what *polite* means to the Colombians — how much formalism, how much etiquette, how much respect, how much emphasis is upon parents, on the elderly, or on social status — we must substitute some lexical meaning given in an English or a Spanish dictionary. Of course, we could obtain the psychological meaning of politeness in turn, but if we were to do that with every response, or even with every response having a high score, we would have to limit our investigations to very circumscribed semantic domains. We have, in the interest of being as broad as possible, relied whenever feasible upon lexical meaning.

A second source of imprecision in dealing with group meaning is that, again, for simple practical reasons we are inclined to adopt another assumption: that the distribution obtained from a group can be considered as being representative of the individual group members. As Deese (1965) has observed, these assumptions are inherent in association norms, yet it is important to keep clearly in mind that the response distributions come from a group, not from a single subject. To take the distributions as characteristic of a person is analogous to describing the characteristics of a single undergraduate at a given college by the average characteristics of all undergraduates of that college. The extent to which such an assumption is valid naturally depends on the homogeneity of subjects or undergraduates. We know that our groups are not always homogeneous and that this assumption may result in certain oversimplifications and distortions. There are two main justifications. First, the method focuses on groups rather than on persons. Second, the amount of distortion that results from the assumption of homogeneity is not entirely a speculative question. It can be measured by a "coefficient of homogeneity," to be discussed later (p. 42).

The content analysis offers several opportunities for distortion. The procedure described earlier in this chapter probably minimizes them, but because they may well enter specific analyses, we shall, wherever possible, present the entire distribution of responses together with the categorical analysis of those responses.

THE NATURE OF DOMINANCE, AFFINITY, AND AFFECTIVITY

We need to say a word about the concepts of dominance, affinity, and affectivity in this methodological context. These notions are not "theoretical constructs" or "intervening variables," nor can they be "operationalized" by some arbitrary fiat. Rather, they simply characterize the major coordinates or dimensions of subjective meaning. The notion of dominance, for example, is chiefly meant to describe the fact that certain themes and even certain domains are more important to a given culture than are other themes and domains. There is no certain or single way to discover that importance. We might suppose that important themes are those that people in a given culture think about and talk about often. In many cases that is true, but in others it is not. Taboo concepts, for example, may almost never be talked about or even thought about and still be central to a culture. The point is that there is never a single way to "measure" dominance. It all depends upon the context. However, it is still true that certain aspects of our behavior and thought processes are more likely than others to reveal the centrality of themes and domains. Thus, having chosen to study cultural meaning through associations, we may use the differential ability of themes and domains to elicit associates easily and rapidly as a way of evaluating the relative dominance of those concepts, so long as we appreciate the fact that such a method should be abandoned on those occasions when context suggests it to be faulty, as in the case of such taboo domains as death and (to a lesser degree nowadays) sex in American culture.

The notion of dominance or salience can only apply to psychological meaning. To be sure, linguistic meaning represents a kind of abstract consensus as to the definition of a concept, but the extent of the consensus or the centrality of the concept to those who provide the consensus is a matter of little or no consequence to the linguist *qua* linguist. He or she could not care less that most Americans use the concept *milk* more often and probably more accurately than they use the concept *claret*. However, anyone who attempts to understand the significance of ideas for particular cultures must know which ideas are important and central to that culture and which are not. Therefore, the notion of dominance is of central importance to psychological meaning.

Dominance

Using the rate at which people produce associates to a given concept as an index of the meaningfulness of that concept to them is well established (Noble, 1952). Accepting the warning that particular contexts may render the technique in error, we find good evidence for the validity of the measure. Noble, in his original investigations, showed that the number of associations generated to a concept in the method of continued association differentiated between two-syllable but uncommon English words and two-syllable nonsense words that obeyed the phonetic rules of English. Furthermore, such phonetically well-structured nonsense words produced more associates than those that were not well-structured, and relatively common English words produced more associates than those that were uncommon.

Since Noble's (1952) investigation, countless studies have demonstrated the validity of associative rate. Concrete words are usually more familiar and central to the thought processes of ordinary people than are abstract words, and, indeed, concrete words usually produce more associations in a fixed period of time than do abstract words. As Noble and others have pointed out, the rate at which associations are generated in the continued-association method declines with the number of associations already given. Therefore, it would be entirely appropriate, as we have done, to weigh earlier associations more heavily than later ones in arriving at an index of dominance for more or less general use. The index we have used in most instances is simply the sum of the individual response scores to a given concept. In comparisons based on groups of equal size, these totals can be directly compared.

We shall demonstrate many examples of the use of a such a dominance score in the cross-cultural and cross-group comparisons that follow. One example, presented here, however, will illustrate what such an index reveals. Szalay and Bryson (1973) compared the dominance scores for a group of young, blue-collar White males and a group of young, blue-collar Black males. First of all, for concepts in general, the dominance scores for Blacks were lower than those for Whites. That cannot, of course, be taken to mean that the concepts examined were more meaningful for Whites than for Blacks. More than likely, it is simply a reflection of the kinds of things that produce similar differences in verbal measures of many sorts — a different attitude towards testing situations, differences in verbal facileness, etc. But when the dominance scores are corrected for this general difference, some interesting variations among themes and domains emerge. The dominance scores for the various "ism" concepts (*democracy, socialism, capitalism, communism*) are higher for Whites than for Blacks. It is not surprising that the dominance scores for concepts centering around racial integration are higher for Blacks than for Whites, but there is an even larger difference in favor of Blacks for such concepts as *goal, expectation, desire*, and *valuable*. Even larger differences occur cross-culturally. For example, in one study, the theme *filial duty* produced a dominance score of 55 for an American sample and a score of 954 for a Korean sample.

Affinity

The relationship of affinity produces a subtler and more difficult problem. It is not that the study of similarity among concepts has not received attention from psychologists. There is a long history of the application of indices of similarity to associative data (see Mackenzie, 1972 for a review and critique of the various indices). Generally, as employed by psychologists, the relationship of similarity has been assumed to be transitive and symmetric. If A is similar to B, then B is to the same degree similar to A. Also, if A is more similar to B than it is to C, then B is more similar to C than A is. Because associations are neither inherently transitive nor symmetric, indices of similarity between distributions of associations have been troublesome. Deese (1965) and others have circumvented this difficulty in a variety of ways, whereas Szalay and his colleagues (e.g., Szalay & Bryson, 1973) have preferred an index that is asymmetric and not necessarily transitive. It should be pointed out that Tversky (1977) has proposed a metric on similarity in which symmetry is not assumed. Because the methods for arriving at indices of affinity and similarity in associations are closely related (the main difference is in the treatment of concepts eliciting each other as associates), the asymmetries are, in practice, small, and the patterns, in any large matrix of concepts, are very much the same whether the index is one using a single symmetric index or one using asymmetric pairs.

In fact, however, any index of similarity or affinity is of limited usefulness in dealing with the structure of psychological meaning. Torgerson (1965), in a discussion of multidimensional scaling, pointed out that metric notions of similarity apply only to certain domains and certain relations within those domains. It makes sense to talk about the similarity between *lions* and *tigers* or between *cheese* and *meat*, but it makes no sense whatever to talk about the similarity between *lions* and *animals* or between *cheese* and *food*.

The reason for the failure of the notion of similarity to apply to all interconcept relations is not hard to find. Similarity, as a metric, makes sense where the relations are created by features shared in common. However, as Aristotle recognized in his analysis of rhetoric, the relation is different when it is one of part—whole or subordinate—supraordinate. To be sure these are logical structures, but they clearly influence and perhaps are also the result of our categories of thought. Casagrande and Hale (1967) pointed out that their Papago informant thought of facial features in terms of location (the nose is that which is between the eyes and the ears), whereas we think of them as being members of an elaborate part—whole structure (the nose is part of the face, the face is part of the head, and the head is part of the body).

Nevertheless, the degree to which associative distributions overlap is a fundamental way of getting at the salience of the variety of relations that link two concepts. These distributions do not reveal some kind of similarity space in the head, but they do tell us something of the extent of relations between concepts. And they reveal important features about the way in which people think of things. For example, Szalay and Bryson (1973) reported that there was no overlap at all in the distributions of response scores to the themes *unemployment* and *expectation* in their White sample, but there was a large and statistically significant overlap in the distributions of associations given by the Blacks.

We make use of several different ways of treating affinal relations among distributions of associations, and so we do not emphasize a particular method here. Once again, we need to point out that overlapping distributions of associations statistically summarize a variety of relations in meaning, some of which will be relations of similarity, but others of which will be relations of coordination, part—whole, subordinate—supraordinate, etc.

To make this nondifferentiating property of overlapping associations clear, we use the term *affinity* to describe such overlapping. We regard affinity, then, as the degree to which persons or groups see relations of any sort between two themes (e.g., *poverty* and *hunger*). Affinity informs about what intrinsic relations, whatever their cause, exist in subjective meaning and their salience in the minds of the respondents. Affinity indices can be used to assess the organization of meaning into domains as well as to describe the relations among such domains (Szalay & Maday, 1973).

Similarity

We hereafter use the term *similarity* to refer to the extent to which two persons or groups think alike about a concept — the agreement in psychological meaning expressed about a concept. For our associative data, such similarity may be evaluated by product-moment correlations between the frequencies of responses or response scores to a given concept. For closely related groups, such correlations will be high, although they will vary from concept to concept. For example, in the norms gathered by Keppel and Strand (1970) from a group of college students using the method of discrete association, the correlations between the frequencies of the various responses to *chair* for men and women was .97. For the same sample, the correlation based upon responses to the word *cut* was only .48. In the latter case, important responses for the women were *scissors* and *finger*, responses hardly given at all by the men. Men and women gave *knife* about equally often, but the men much more often produced *blood*. In order to obtain a negative or zero correlation for men and women in the same culture, it would probably be necessary to sample heavily in the domain of sex roles.

The correlations presented in Table 2.6 demonstrate the usefulness of such an index of similarity in cross-cultural studies. These correlations come from student, working-class, and farmer samples obtained in the United States and in Korea. The correlations are based upon response scores.

The results show substantial intracultural similarities but very few cross-cultural similarities in both domains. Table 2.7 shows mean correlations (based on Z transformations) for nine domains comparing Korean and American samples. The patterns revealed in detail for two domains in Table 2.6 are repeated in all nine domains. In fact, the cross-similarities are greater for the domains of *family* and *education* than for the others.

Affectivity

In the first chapter we pointed out that most things human beings commonly think about have either positive or negative affective connotations. In order to estimate the affectivity of the reactions to associative stimuli, we have, where interest warrants, asked judges to sort the responses into three categories: positive, negative, and neutral. An index of affectivity is arrived at by summing the scores of positively coded responses, dividing by the total possible score, and multiplying by 100. The result is an index that can vary from +100 to −100. Scores near the neutral point are sometimes ambiguous. That is, they could result from there being a large number of neutral items or from many positive responses being offset by many negative responses. Therefore, in some cases we shall want to know something about the distribution of positive, negative, and neutral judgments so that we can evaluate the extent to which ambivalence is present.

Given the propositional interpretation of the nature of associations, adjective or attribute-named responses became particularly important in determining the affectivity of the stimulus. An attribute given as an association to a word indicates that the person so responding believes that attribute to be descriptive of the stimulus word. Therefore, once again as interest warrants, it may be worthwhile to tabulate an affectivity score for the adjectival or attributional responses separately. That has been done in Table 2.8, which exhibits affectivity indices

TABLE 2.6
Coefficients of Intergroup Associative Similarity on
Themes of the Domains *Family* and *Education*

| | Similarities Within Cultures | | | | | | Similarities Between Cultures | | |
| | Between U.S. Groups | | | Between Korean Groups | | | U.S. – Korean | | |
Themes	S and W[a]	S and F[b]	W and F	S and F	S and F	W and F	S	W	F
Family	.84	.81	.89	.87	.86	.94	.51	.68	.58
Love	.85	.88	.89	.55	.62	.75	-.02	.10	.00
Father	.68	.71	.67	.77	.74	.79	.27	.42	.06
Mother	.79	.84	.88	.90	.90	.90	.71	.52	.59
Me	.56	.40	.63	.73	.85	.85	-.20	-.11	-.04
Relatives	.80	.74	.83	.83	.81	.86	.57	.64	.37
Ancestor	.80	.75	.89	.61	.47	.67	.04	.10	.07
Filial duty	.89	.84	.91	-.18	-.07	.47	.06	-.23	-.24
Authority	.31	.27	.27	.36	.29	.75	.06	-.08	-.32
Respect	.81	.73	.74	.49	.43	.73	.08	.11	.15
Mean r[c]	.77	.74	.81	.67	.68	.80	.22	.25	.15
Educated	.52	.60	.60	.58	.64	.82	.13	-.08	-.14
Knowledge	.59	.54	.81	.54	.61	.80	.60	.37	.55
Intelligence	.61	.56	.69	.64	.65	.95	.41	-.09	-.14
To learn	.80	.70	.84	.59	.67	.71	.50	.66	.60
College	.53	.55	.79	.73	.75	.91	.10	.14	.20
School	.89	.88	.87	.77	.71	.77	.57	.71	.50
Teacher	.66	.67	.84	.67	.65	.71	.35	.33	.29
Degree	.67	.74	.77	.84	.83	.75	.11	-.10	-.00
Mean r	.69	.67	.79	.68	.70	.83	.37	.28	.25

[a] S = students, W = workers.
[b] F = farmers.
[c] Mean *r*s based on *Z* transformation.

TABLE 2.7

Similarities across Domains within and between U.S. and Korean Culture Groups

Domains	Themes	Similarities Within Cultures						Similarities Between Cultures		
		Between U.S. Groups			Between Korean Groups			U.S. – Korean Groups		
		S and W[a]	S and F[b]	W and F	S and W	S and F	W and F	S	W	F
Family	10	.77	.74	.81	.67	.68	.80	.22	.25	.15
Education	8	.69	.67	.79	.68	.70	.83	.37	.28	.25
Ethics, morality	12	.54	.55	.68	.48	.49	.60	.00	−.23	−.23
Economy, finances	8	.70	.65	.78	.71	.69	.81	.24	.13	.00
International relations	12	.60	.50	.62	.55	.56	.76	.09	−.08	−.12
Social	8	.48	.45	.57	.51	.59	.65	.00	−.04	−.12
Political	12	.57	.57	.64	.70	.69	.77	.12	−.04	−.04
National	12	.65	.59	.77	.58	.58	.55	.06	−.13	−.07
Goals, concerns	8	.59	.54	.78	.46	.46	.64	−.01	−.16	−.14
Average across domains		.64	.59	.71	.60	.61	.72	.12	.02	−.04

[a] S = students, W = workers.
[b] F = farmers.

45

TABLE 2.8
Evaluative Indices Based on All Responses and on Adjective Responses
Obtained to 15 Stimulus Words from Three Cultural Groups

Stimulus Word	U.S. Group		Korean Group		Colombian Group	
	All Responses	Adjective Responses	All Responses	Adjective Responses	All Responses	Adjective Responses
Hungry	−27	−88	−26	−92	−32	−84
Rice	− 2	18	1	−21	6	35
Poor	−58	−70	−28	−67	−40	−86
Beggar	−63	−92	−42	−89	− 8	−86
Family	25	73	22	77	20	48
Ancestors	9	−31	13	16	6	−26
Educated	51	95	51	94	44	84
Proud	12	−20	28	77	−26	−50
Offense	−27	−70	−53	−70	−64	−68
Revenge	−70	−95	−49	−59	−58	−75
Capitalism	10	60	− 4	−11	1	− 6
Socialism	4	−10	11	8	3	−31
Communism	−14	−48	−32	−91	−20	−57
Knowledge	50	83	44	78	33	44
Equality	20	29	19	78	25	62

for some selected concepts given by respondants in three cultures, American, Korean, and Colombian.

Notice that there is considerably more agreement among the three cultures in the extent and direction of affectivity for these concepts than we might have expected, given the divergencies in intergroup associative similarity. This result is, however, in accordance with the results of cross-cultural studies using the semantic differential (Osgood, 1964).

RELIABILITY OF DATA

Finally, in this chapter generally devoted to methodological matters, we need to give some attention to questions of reliability and the determination of the statistical significance of particular results. Although we cannot solve all of the problems associated with particular results to be presented later, we can establish certain general standards for the assessment of results and can point out, by reference to reliability studies, the general stability of patterns in associations.

Perhaps the simplest and most straightforward question we can ask is: How often will a response, once given to a particular stimulus by a particular individual, recur when the same individual is tested with the same word? The data upon which the weighting technique is based (Table 2.1), show the answer to be about 32% of the time. This figure, of course, will vary according to the stimulus word, the person, and probably the conditions of testing. However, it gives us a point of reference against which to judge the stability of group scores. Comparing two groups of 50 persons each with a sample of words similar to those used in the earlier study (see Table 2.1) resulted in an average figure of 62%. That is, a randomly selected group of 50 individuals gave an average of 62% responses to each of those words that were the same as the responses given by another randomly selected group of 50 individuals. Such a figure, such as the one for the average individual, is, of course, dependent upon the particular stimulus, the degree of cultural homogeneity of the sample, etc.

We have attempted to provide some baseline for the homogeneity of a reference sample (United States) by randomly splitting a sample of 100 persons twice. We then calculated similarity indices (product-moment correlations) for each of the two random splits for all 26 stimuli. The average correlation difference between the two samples was .047. The largest difference (to the stimulus concept, *McGovern*) was .13, whereas half of the words produced a difference in correlation of less than .03. The highest pair of correlations resulted from the stimulus *family* (.89, .87) and the lowest for the stimulus *Spanish-American* (.50, .48). Therefore, this sample was relatively homogeneous in its interpretation of the concept *family* but remarkably heterogeneous in its interpretation of the concept *Spanish-American*. This, of course, reminds us of an important aspect of cross-cultural comparisons. We can only speak of cultural homogeneity or heterogeneity with respect to something. It would be surprising to find any group of individuals who were homogeneous in their thinking about all concepts.

A word about statistical comparisons between groups is in order. Frequencies of a particular response to a particular stimulus create no problems. Subjects do not repeat their responses; so, in a frequency count, each response comes from a different individual. Therefore, simple chi-square comparisons can be made. Or, if response scores are at issue, they can be transformed into frequencies simply by dividing by the mean response score. We have calculated score value differences required for significance at the .05 and .01 levels for various sample sizes used in the investigations reported in later chapters. These provide the significance levels reported for cross-cultural and cross-group comparisons of particular themes.

Within-group comparisons, however, cannot be made in the same way, because here the numbers do not come from independent groups of subjects. If, for example, we want to know whether the theme *equality* produces more responses, *women*, than *Blacks*, we must resort to other methods. A convenient reference point is the test–retest difference to the same words. To provide a standard of comparison, 50 American subjects were tested and retested again 3 months later on the same words. The standard deviation of the mean difference, excluding idiosyncratic responses, was 7.0. If this is a stable figure, and there is reason to believe that it is, a difference of 14 between two different words from the same sample of 50 subjects would exceed chance variation at the .05 level, and a score difference of 18 would exceed chance at the .01 level. In the example above, *equality* elicited *women* with a score of 16 and *Blacks* with a score of 39. This is a difference of 23, in excess of 18. Such comparisons, however, are critically dependent upon the samples of words and subjects. They cannot be regarded as tests of significance so much as points of reference for differences under the assumption that the particular sample under consideration resembles the reference sample. A similar analysis may be provided for whole domains.

Wherever possible, however, we assess the statistical significance of results by tests based upon independent frequencies. For example, the category scores are based upon a coding of underlying responses. If there is a statistically reliable difference between frequencies underlying a category for two different groups, we may assume that the category itself is different for the groups. Where we cannot do that, we resort to various nonparametric comparisons, and where that is impossible we try to evaluate a result by comparison with some obtained result based upon chance variation.

3 National and Group Images

The notion of image in the sense of "national image" or "the image of the President" grows out of pop sociology. It is, nevertheless, a useful idea, despite its connotations of manipulation and vulgar distortion of the democratic process. It is an example of what we have called a *representational process*. That is, it is a portrayal of the structured, subjective reaction characteristic of some group of individuals towards some significant concept.

A KOREAN-AMERICAN COMPARISON

The ability of an associational analysis to detect the main outlines of such images is revealed in a comparative study of Korean and American attitudes (Szalay, Moon, Lysne, & Bryson, 1971; Szalay, Moon, & Bryson, 1973), and a recapitulation of that study provides a convenient beginning for this chapter. The data produced in this comparison were obtained in an effort to determine the national images of the United States, Japan, South Vietnam, the Soviet Union, and Red China possessed by Korean and American samples.

Data Collection

The data were obtained during the summer of 1968. The American sample was from new Army recruits, tested on their arrival at four basic training centers (Fort Ord, Fort Dix, Fort Leonard Wood, and Fort Jackson). The Korean sample was from the South Korean national training camp at Nonsan. The association tests were given during a period devoted to the standard paper-and-pencil tests used by both armies. The subjects were selected at random upon their arrival at the training center. From a larger group of subjects (1,600 American and 300 Koreans), it was possible to pick three occupational groups (students, urban workers, and farmers) of 50 each by random selection on the basis of a background questionnaire (U.S.) and personal data files (Korea). The age of the subjects varied between 19.5 and 22.9 years. All the Korean subjects and between 70 and 80% of the U.S. subjects were single. The U.S. subjects were mostly Protestants and Catholics; most of the Korean subjects identified themselves as having no formal religious affiliation. In income the majority of the American sample fell into the $4,000 to $10,000 range, and the majority of the Korean into the $480 to $1,200 range. In general, the samples were representative of the general U.S. and Korean male populations in this age bracket.

Stimulus themes were selected on the basis of previous test results, the advice of cultural experts, and a study of the literature on intercultural communications. Korean area experts assisted in the identification of special problems likely to be important in American–Korean communications. Themes administered in English to Americans and in Korean to Koreans were chosen to represent the closest available translation-equivalents. In identifying the closest available equivalents (which were not always very close), the advice of Korean language experts was sought, and back-translations by Korean–English bilinguals were employed.

Components of Meaning

Figure 3.1 shows the main components of both the American and Korean image of Americans. The American subjects responded much more characteristically with components centering on *nation, country,* and *inhabitants* than did the Koreans. *Freedom* and *democracy* were important components for the Americans and their self-image contained strong, positive personal attributes (*good*), a reference to *economic well being*, and elements dealing with the *military*. Nearly half of the Korean responses to *Americans* identified *physical features. Color* and *physiognomy* reflected a focus on ethnic and racial features. The body size of Americans (*tall, big*) emerged in distinct contrast to the Korean's self-image as *short.* Americans were characterized as being *good, great,* and *gentle,* but their outstanding characteristic was *richness.* The components *alliance* and *friendship* appeared for the Koreans but not for the Americans.

Table 3.1 shows some of the particular responses that made up some of these categories, as well as a few others where the responses themselves reveal some of the differences between the groups. Notice that the Koreans perceived Americans as being both *White* and *Black*, although, not unexpectedly, *White* responses were more numerous. The Korean students even occasionally responded with *Yellow.*

A very similar pattern held for the concept *United States.* For the American group, this particular concept brought out a much stronger *military* component

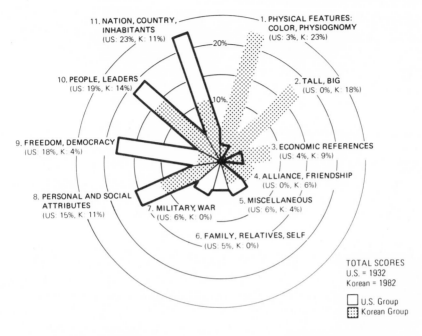

11. NATION, COUNTRY, INHABITANTS (US: 23%, K: 11%)

1. PHYSICAL FEATURES: COLOR, PHYSIOGNOMY (US: 3%, K: 23%)

10. PEOPLE, LEADERS (US: 19%, K: 14%)

2. TALL, BIG (US: 0%, K: 18%)

9. FREEDOM, DEMOCRACY (US: 18%, K: 4%)

3. ECONOMIC REFERENCES (US: 4%, K: 9%)

4. ALLIANCE, FRIENDSHIP (US: 0%, K: 6%)

8. PERSONAL AND SOCIAL ATTRIBUTES (US: 15%, K: 11%)

5. MISCELLANEOUS (US: 6%, K: 4%)

7. MILITARY, WAR (US: 6%, K: 0%)

6. FAMILY, RELATIVES, SELF (US: 5%, K: 0%)

20%

10%

TOTAL SCORES
U.S. = 1932
Korean = 1982

☐ U.S. Group
▦ Korean Group

U.S. GROUPS

Identification with their own NATION, COUNTRY, INHABITANTS, and with the PEOPLE, LEADERS, are the most sizable elements of the Americans' self-image—reflecting a populist, democratic frame of reference. They see FREEDOM as the single, outstanding attribute of AMERICANS. This self-image also contains strong, positive PERSONAL ATTRIBUTES (good), ECONOMIC REFERENCES (richness), and elements dealing with the MILITARY (armed forces in particular).

KOREAN GROUPS

Nearly half of the Korean responses involve the PHYSICAL FEATURES of AMERICANS. COLOR and PHYSIOGNOMY reflect a focus on distinctive ethnic-racial features. The body size of the Americans—TALL, BIG—emerges in distinct contrast with the Koreans' self-image as short (see analysis of the theme, OWN PEOPLE). In respect to PERSONAL AND SOCIAL ATTRIBUTES, Americans are characterized as good, great, gentle. Richness is their most salient ECONOMIC REFERENCE. Furthermore, ALLIANCE, FRIENDSHIP characterize the American-Korean relationship.

FIG. 3.1. A graphic representation of the main components of the meaning of the concept *American* for Americans and Koreans.

than did *Americans. Political institutions,* especially *government,* occurred for both Koreans and Americans. Once again, *richness* and *wealth* were important components in the Korean conception. There was a notable absence of the possible response *capitalism* (and its allied responses) for the Koreans. This may have been the result of the generally favorable attitude of the Koreans towards the United States. It is an attitude apparently unlike that in many newly independent, developing countries, which equate colonialism with capitalism (Sigmund, 1963). *Size,* both of the individuals and of the country, was clearly

TABLE 3.1
Reactions in Selected Components by Korean and American Recruits towards the Concept *Americans*

	Response Scores[a]							
	U.S. Groups				*Korean Groups*			
Reactions	*S*	*W*	*F*	*Total*	*S*	*W*	*F*	*Total*
1. Physical features								
Healthy	10	–	–	10	–	–	–	–
Variety	14	–	–	14	–	–	–	–
White	–	–	10	10	43	43	24	110
Black	–	–	–	–	10	16	8	34
Yellow	–	–	–	–	12	–	–	12
Eyes, blue eyes	–	–	–	–	21	13	11	45
Hair, blond hair	–	–	–	–	6	20	30	56
Body structure	–	–	–	–	9	–	6	15
Nose, big nose	–	–	–	–	70	51	46	167
Misc.[b]	17	7	–	24	6	–	9	15
2. Size								
Tall, stature	–	–	–	–	112	112	92	316
Big (body)	–	–	–	–	23	13	6	42
Giant	–	–	–	–	10	–	–	10
3. People, leaders								
People	90	109	155	354	33	31	63	127
Men	–	11	9	20	–	–	–	–
Kennedy	–	–	–	–	15	31	14	60
L. B. Johnson	–	–	–	–	11	22	20	53
Lincoln	–	–	–	–	–	11	–	11
Misc.[c]	–	–	–	–	–	29	–	20
4. Personal and social attributes								
Friendly, Friend	–	10	20	30	–	–	–	–
Helpful, Help	8	9	15	32	–	–	–	–
Happy, Happiness	17	10	10	37	–	–	–	–
Honest, Honesty	–	10	8	18	–	–	–	–
Pride, Proud	16	7	12	35	–	–	–	–
Good, Best, Great	5	19	26	50	19	17	18	54
Society	10	–	–	10	–	–	–	–
Sincerity	–	–	–	–	–	–	10	10
Gentle, Gentleness	–	–	–	–	11	17	10	38
Strong	9	12	6	27	–	–	–	10
Senseless	–	–	–	–	12	–	–	12

[a]S = students, W = workers, F = farmers.
[b]Clean, different diverse (U.S.), leg (Korean).
[c]McNamara, Nixon, Eisenhower, Edison (Korean).

an important component of the reactions of the Koreans. The Koreans identified *democracy* with the United States more strongly than *freedom*. This greater emphasis upon *democracy* in their perception of many countries (including their own) is characteristic of the Korean groups.

The image of the United States in terms of political institutions was, for Americans, strongly tied up with the concept of *government,* whereas for the Koreans there was a strong component of people, such as *Kennedy* and *Johnson. Kennedy* was a strong component of *Americans* and the *United States* for these Koreans, even 5 years after his assassination.

The Korean image of Japan has emotional roots in the past. Not surprisingly, an important component of *Japan* for the Koreans was *Japanese rule.* The Koreans agreed with the Americans in having a strong component of *war* and *militarism* for *Japan* (United States, 16%; Korean, 12% of the total response scores). Again, not surprisingly, the physical characteristics of the Japanese (*size, eye shape*) were more important for the Americans than for the Koreans, whereas the Koreans were more concerned with Japanese attitudes and intentions.

The reactions *neighbor* and *neutral,* which were both strong responses for the Koreans, tell us something about the nature of contemporary Korean—Japanese relations. Japan is obviously important for Korea, both because of its proximity and strength. However, the Koreans appeared to think of Japan as being more of a neutral nation than a friendly one. This conception, of course, has a powerful historical background, beginning with the repressive Japanese occupation, continuing with Japan's reluctance to be involved in the Korean War, Japan's disregard for the South Korean government's proposal for the repatriation of Korean residents, and the anti-Japanese campaign under Rhee (Lee Hahn-been, 1968). These responses tend to support the observations by Ray (1965) and Lee Young Ho (1972) that the Koreans generally distrust Japan. On an affectivity dimension, the Koreans score rather heavily on the negative side in their attitude towards Japan. Such notions as *strong* and *cunning,* in this context, have negative connotations, and the Koreans use the word *woenom,* (dwarfish Japanese — an ethnic pejorative).

People was a stronger component of Japan for Americans than for Koreans (14% of the total as opposed to 2%, respectively). There were many responses of *woman, girl,* and *Geisha,* on the part of the Americans and only a few such responses from the Korean students. The dense population of Japan was perceived by the Americans and revealed in such responses as *population, overpopulated,* and *crowded.* These responses did not occur at all for the Koreans.

These data were obtained at the very height of the war in South Vietnam, and the dominance of that war in the minds of the young American recruits is not surprising. Thirty-eight percent of the responses of the Americans to *South Vietnam* centered in a *war* and *killing* component, whereas only 12% of the Korean responses centered in this component. There were a significant number of negative references in the responses of the Americans (6%) and none at all in the Korean responses. *Military, climate,* or *location,* were, surprisingly, more dominant components for the Koreans than for the Americans. The *military* responses for the Koreans were generally positive. Specific responses referred to the *Tiger,* the *White Horse Divisions,* and the *Blue Dragon Division,* etc., elite groups of Korean troops who fought with the Americans in Vietnam. For the Koreans at this time, participation in the war seemed to connote national pride and prestige. The *military* responses of the Americans centered, not surprisingly, around *Army,* with only scattered reference to the Marines. The specific *climate* and *location* responses were similar for the Americans and the Koreans. *Heat* and the *jungle* were mentioned by both, whereas Americans gave *rice-paddies* and Koreans gave *coconut tree* and *banana.*

Unlike the Koreans, the Americans gave many affectively negative responses to South Vietnam. *Death, dead,* and *die* occurred commonly for the Americans (response score of 109), whereas these hardly occurred at all for the Koreans (response score of 9). Not surprisingly, Americans more often gave responses centering on the components *poor, small,* and *backward,* but there were also responses centering on *alliance* and *friendship.* These latter responses, in fact occurred more commonly for the Americans than for the Koreans.

There was surprising concurrence in the American and Korean views of the Soviet Union. The only large discrepancy was in the component *country* or *nation.* The Americans were very much aware of the Soviet Union as being *Russian,* and the Koreans were much less concerned with this specific component. There was a stronger emphasis upon *leaders* for the Koreans than for the Americans. Both placed emphasis upon such physical features as *large* and *cold.* For both the Koreans and the Americans, the chief component of the concept *Soviet Union* was *communism–socialism.* The Koreans, however, separated *communism* and *socialism.* The Americans did not. The affective reaction of both the Koreans and the Americans was negative, with such specific responses as *bad, powerful,* and *savage* (Korean), *stupid* and *crazy* (American). Both samples agreed upon a component of *despotism* and *lack of freedom.* Finally, both American and Koreans regarded the Soviet Union as a formidable country – *might, powerful, strong, dangerous,* a *menace,* and a *threat.*

Communism also played a salient role in the conception of Red China held by these samples of Koreans and Americans. The other salient component for Americans was *war* and *militarism,* whereas the other salient feature for the Koreans was provided by the component of *leadership* personified by *Mao-tse-tung. Poverty* and *hunger* occurred for the Americans but hardly at all for the Koreans. Both the Koreans and Americans thought of people in connection with Red China as *masses.* The idea of *hostility* and *threat* showed greater salience for Americans than for Koreans. The Koreans showed a preoccupation with lack of *freedom* and with *compulsory labor,* notions not occurring in the responses of the Americans. The *Republic of China* (Taiwan) *U.S.S.R., North Korea,* and *Japan* all occurred as responses for the Koreans, but for the Americans it was

Russia and *Vietnam* that predominated. There were negatively affective responses for both American and Koreans, but they were much more prominent for the Americans. *Bad, dangerous, crazy, crowded* were all responses of Americans. *Savage* was the only considerable negative response for the Koreans.

Many of the components of these concepts would doubtless be different if testing occurred in 1977. The end of the Vietnam War has left a legacy in American life, but nonetheless, the fact that it has ended means that there must be some shifts in American attitudes towards not only South Vietnam but the whole international constellation. Surely, the dramatic reopening of relations with China should also change certain components of the reactions to it and other countries. We can be less sure about Korean conceptions, but as the Rhee era recedes in time, surely some of the negativism and conservatism shall also recede as well as attitudes towards Japan and communism.

AN EXAMPLE OF ETHNIC AND RACIAL IMAGES

Data Collection

An investigation of ethnic and racial images is illustrated by a study of Black, White, and Spanish-speaking students in the Washington, D.C. area. In this study, each group was represented by a sample of 50 students (25 male and 25 female). The White students came from the University of Maryland at College Park, and the Black group from students at the District of Columbia Teacher's College. The Spanish-speaking students were tested at American University; they included students from various universities and colleges in the Washington area. The majority were Spanish-Americans, but there were students from Latin America as well.

In order to establish some notion as to how these groups regarded one another independently of the association test, the students were asked to evaluate each

TABLE 3.2

Affective Ratings of *Me, Blacks, Whites,* and *Spanish-Americans* by Samples (N = 50 each) of Black, White, and Spanish-Speaking Students

	Mean Ratings			
Group	*Me*	*Blacks*	*Whites*	*Spanish-Americans*
Blacks	2.4	2.4	−0.7	0.4
Whites	2.0	0.7	1.4	0.2
Spanish-Americans	2.4	1.2	1.1	2.2

Note. All differences were significant at the .01 level except the White–Spanish-American difference for Whites and the Black–White difference for Spanish-Americans.

stimulus theme positively or negatively and to indicate the strength of their evaluation on a 3-point scale (1 = slight, 2 = medium, 3 = strong). Table 3.2 gives the results of these ratings for the concepts *me, Blacks, Whites,* and *Spanish-Americans.* The results are not surprising. The only mean negative ratings were for the Black students evaluating the concept *Whites.* Interestingly enough, the White students showed the least positive ratings for *me* and for their own racial designation. The Spanish-speaking students evaluated both *Blacks* and *Whites* positively and to about the same degree. Our main interest, however, centers in the context these ratings provide for associational responses to these concepts.

Components of Meaning

Tables 3.3, 3.4, and 3.5 show the chief components of meaning for the concepts *Blacks, Whites,* and *Spanish-Americans* achieved by the three groups. We have not presented the data on the concept *me;* however, the single most frequent response to *me* was *Black.* Neither the White students nor the Spanish-speaking students thought of themselves primarily in terms of race. For the White and Spanish-Speaking students, there was a strong emphasis on the component *ego,* a response class that was infrequent for the Black students. The strongest identity component for the Spanish-speaking students, however, was a role (e.g., *student, worker*). Both the Black and White students showed a higher score for *feelings* and *moods* than did the Spanish-speaking students.

TABLE 3.3
Meaning Components and Frequent Responses for the Concept *Black*
Given by Samples of Black, White, and Spanish-Speaking Students

	Response Scores		
Components and Responses	*Black*	*White*	*Spanish-Speaking*
People	137	197	98
People	19	35	14
Race	26	31	50
Negroes	21	34	—
Me	23	—	—
Black student union	—	12	—
Group	3	13	—
Minority	14	7	—
Human beings	6	6	17
Friends	—	21	11
Roommate	—	11	—
Families	16	3	—
Athlete	—	10	6

(continued)

TABLE 3.3 *(continued)*

Components and Responses	Response Scores		
	Black	*White*	*Spanish-Speaking*
Origin	20	44	60
Africa	–	21	45
Afro-American	15	22	–
U.S.	5	1	15
Positive characteristics	87	27	31
Beautiful	48	9	7
Good	10	6	16
Hardworking	13	–	–
Negative characteristics	56	61	52
Dumb	13	–	–
Inferior	–	5	10
Life style	19	27	41
Rhythmical	3	3	11
Soul	16	12	–
Whites	16	114	118
Group consciousness	54	57	47
Unity	7	16	–
Togetherness	11	6	–
Strong	10	–	10
Pride, proud	12	17	31
Social ideals	47	24	37
Equality	10	10	27
Freedom	18	9	–
Justice	–	2	10
Love	19	3	–
Discrimination	85	162	177
Racism	8	31	11
Prejudice	6	54	15
Discrimination	22	10	30
Exploitation	15	–	25
Slavery	16	13	16
Oppression	13	21	12
Injustice	–	5	27
Segregation	5	14	21
Social problems	94	93	54
Problems	4	7	21
Welfare	6	10	–
Poor, poverty	34	19	28
Ghetto	7	27	–
Riots	–	15	–
Crime	13	2	–
Education	15	4	–
Total main components	615	802	715
Miscellaneous responses	62	46	54
Total response scores	677	852	769

For the concept *Blacks,* the largest component for the Black students was represented by *people.* This was also the case for the White students, but the specific responses reveal underlying differences. *Me* was a typical response for Black students, whereas White students gave such responses as *athlete, friend, roommate.* Both the Spanish-speaking students and the White students achieved higher scores on the component *discrimination* than did the Black students. For the Black students, negative components were heavily outweighed by posi-

TABLE 3.4

Meaning Components and Frequent Responses for the Concept *White*
Given by Samples of Black, White, and Spanish-Speaking Students

Components and Responses	Response Scores		
	Black	*White*	*Spanish-Speaking*
Race, ethnicity	58	91	124
Race	32	35	48
Americans	−	−	13
Caucasians	16	22	−
Europe	−	8	22
Indians	−	3	10
Indo-European	−	−	10
WASP	−	16	−
People	61	152	53
People	42	59	10
Men	3	6	11
Me	−	63	20
Human	−	7	12
Positive characteristics	29	23	29
Good	25	14	10
Intelligence	4	−	10
Negative characteristics	103	47	28
Bad	28	10	14
Hate	19	9	−
Selfish	12	3	−
Stupid	10	1	−
Unjust	3	−	14
Physical characteristics	−	31	23
Blonde	−	3	10
Eyes, blue/brown	−	18	4
Skin	−	10	−
Blacks	19	150	116
Money	60	31	20
Money	12	6	7
Rich	23	−	6
Wealthy	8	14	−
Jobs	10	4	−

(continued)

TABLE 3.4 *(continued)*

	Response Scores		
Components and Responses	*Black*	*White*	*Spanish-Speaking*
Superiority	73	107	80
Superiority	13	24	22
Supremacy	4	20	–
Power	15	21	22
Aggressive	10	–	–
Dominant	–	3	10
Majority	9	32	9
Prejudice	132	112	86
Prejudice	72	52	19
Discrimination	19	9	20
Racism	23	28	26
Segregation	3	3	21
Bigot	13	10	–
Biased	11	3	–
Total main components	535	744	561
Miscellaneous responses	37	60	79
Total response scores	572	804	638

tive ones, whereas for the Spanish-speaking and White students, positive responses were about the same as negative ones.

For both the concept *Blacks* and *Whites,* the White and Spanish-speaking students were willing to identify a strong *Black–White* polarity, whereas the Black students did not. This does not mean, of course, that the Black students did not perceive a polarity in American society, but they were more sensitive to the nuances of the polarity than were either the White or Spanish-speaking students.

Identity for the Black students was tied more closely to being Black than was being White for the White students or speaking Spanish in a predominantly English-speaking city was for the Spanish students. The *Black–White* polarity was simpler for the Spanish-speaking and White Anglo students. It was just that: a *Black–White* dichotomy. The Black students, of course, were the ones who know what it is to be *Black*, and they were not content with saying that being *Black* is different from being *White*. They knew about *welfare, poverty, drugs,* and *soul,* and these came to mind when they were asked to think about their Blackness. These things, of course, are known from the outside by White Americans, and they come to their minds too, but with less salience. They are secondary to the overwhelming fact of the *Black–White* contrast. We return to this matter of contrast through polarity later.

Blacks were more obviously ambivalent about themselves than were the White or Spanish-speaking students. They gave many more positive responses to *Blacks* than did the White students or Spanish speakers, but they gave just about as

TABLE 3.5
Meaning Components and Frequent Responses for the Concept
Spanish-American Given by Samples of Black, White, and
Spanish-Speaking Students

	Response Scores		
Components and Responses	*Black*	*White*	*Spanish-Speaking*
People	129	225	112
Race	14	6	–
Chicanos	6	26	–
Mexican-Americans	4	23	8
Latins	–	18	23
Spics	–	58	–
Migrant workers	–	72	–
Foreigners	15	9	–
Minority	34	25	–
Friend	13	14	43
Me	–	–	23
People	43	24	–
Countries	66	139	164
America	15	–	5
Mexico	–	26	–
Latin America	–	14	–
Argentina	–	–	12
Cuba	6	15	28
Puerto Rico	21	51	16
South America	–	–	11
Spain	24	21	–
Venezuela	–	–	23
Discrimination	65	45	25
Prejudice	6	18	5
Discrimination	13	5	–
Exploitation	14	4	12
Oppressed	23	12	–
Culture	92	147	76
Culture	–	16	17
Customs	11	3	–
Espanol	4	11	–
Language	31	31	–
Accent	1	19	–
Music	5	7	13
War	13	27	–
Physical characteristics	16	59	–
Dark skin	–	38	–
Hair, long/fine	10	5	–
Positive characteristics	63	26	100
Beautiful	8	10	–
Friendly	8	6	18

(continued)

TABLE 3.5 *(continued)*

Components and Responses	Response Scores		
	Black	White	Spanish-Speaking
Good	4	–	11
Happy	–	3	34
O.K.	12	–	–
Romantic	–	–	11
Understanding	11	5	–
Ideals	21	21	14
Education	14	18	–
Poverty	71	94	27
Poor, poverty	33	38	19
Ghetto	3	11	–
Unemployment	–	11	–
Jobs	16	8	–
Problems	19	–	–
Ignorance	–	13	–
Total main components	523	756	518
Miscellaneous responses	22	32	62
Total response scores	545	788	580

many negative responses. The negative responses were scattered, so except for *dumb,* they do not appear in Table 3.3. However, such responses as *bad, ignorant, stupid,* and *fight* appeared more often for Black students than for White students (a total response score of 23 for Black students as opposed to 12 for White students). These kinds of responses reflect the truest tragedy of racism, the inevitable acceptance on the part of Blacks, however irrational and self-defeating, of at least some of the prejudicial image of *Blacks* held by their White peers. It also could be said that the Blacks were even more prejudiced against the Whites than the Whites were against them. Such a fact, however, has to be judged in the context of the overwhelming power of the White population. A sense of powerlessness along with the residual of the White image of Blacks can easily be seen in the responses of the Black students to the concept *Blacks.*

Our Spanish-speaking students were probably less aware, as a group, of their own special identity than would be Spanish-speaking students from elsewhere in the United States. There are now three main streams of Hispanic culture in the United States: the Southwestern culture, commonly called Chicano; the Puerto Rican culture, centered in the big cities of the Northeast; and the Cuban culture, centered in Miami. Washington, in a sense, is both a meeting ground for these cultures and a polyglot society in its own right, containing Spanish-speaking peoples literally from around the globe. The diversity in our Spanish-speaking sample undoubtedly deemphasized the special contrast Chicano or Puerto Rican culture might have made with Anglo and Black culture in the responses of our Spanish-speaking sample. These students did not give *Chicano* at all as a response,

TABLE 3.6

Correlations in Responses of Black, White, and Spanish-Speaking
Students to the Concepts *Black, White,* and *Spanish-Americans*

	Concepts					
	Black		*White*		*Spanish-American*	
	n	*r*	*n*	*r*	*n*	*r*
Total response scores						
Black–White	79	.176	61	.397***	61	.119
Black–Spanish	73	.097	63	.227**	73	−.214***
Spanish–White	78	.675***	65	.781***	80	−.136
Response components						
Positive and negative affect						
Black–White	19	.036	13	.521*	9	.161
Black–Spanish	18	−.437*	13	.233	12	−.612*
Spanish–White	17	−.421*	13	−.082	10	−.612
Problems plus poverty						
Black–White	20	.032	–	–	12	.124
Black–Spanish	16	.195	–	–	11	.084
Spanish–White	19	.064	–	–	12	.061
Money and power						
Black–White	–	–	15	.946	–	–
Black–Spanish	–	–	17	.196	–	–
Spanish–White	–	–	15	.419*	–	–

*p between .10 and .05.   ***$p < .01$.
**$p \leqslant .05$.

although it occurred in the responses of both Black and White students. The
Spanish speakers gave *Latin* as their chief ethnic designation. Few gave *New York*
as a response to *Spanish-American,* although many of the Black and White students did. Incidentally, it should be noted that while racial epithets for Blacks
were only infrequently used by the White students (*nigger* had a response score
of only 8), the White students freely used the epithet *spic* in response to *Spanish-
Americans* (response score of 58).

Table 3.6 reveals the patterns of similarities and differences among the images
of the three concepts *Blacks, Whites,* and *Spanish-Americans,* possessed by
these three groups. There was more agreement about the concept White than
about the others, and the Spanish-speaking and White students agreed more
closely about the concepts *Blacks* and *Whites* than did the Black and White or
Black and Spanish-speaking students. There was less agreement about *Spanish-
Americans* than about the other two concepts. Very clearly, these groups had very
different images of *Spanish-Americans.* In fact, the correlations for the response
distributions in the Black–Spanish-speaking and White–Spanish-speaking com-

parisons were negative. In the specific components, the Spanish-speaking students did not agree at all with the Black and White students in affective meaning. The correlations were negative for the concepts *Blacks* and *Spanish-Americans* and close to zero for the concept *Whites*. All three groups revealed a concern for problems of *poverty* and *discrimination* for the *Blacks* and *Spanish-Americans*, but the specific responses were very different. The correlations were all close to zero. *Poverty* and *hunger* were salient for Black students about *Blacks,* but *riots* and *prejudice* were salient for White students about *Blacks*. The Spanish-speaking students saw *Spanish-Americans* as much less subject to discrimination and problems of poverty than did the Black and White students. The total response scores in the *social problems* component for *Spanish-Americans* was 52 for the Spanish-speaking students as opposed to 136 for the Black students and 139 for the White students. Once again, this is a reflection of the special nature of these Spanish-speaking students. The Black and White students appeared to be thinking of Puerto Ricans and Chicanos, whereas the Spanish-speaking students were thinking of Latin America.

These patterns reveal the complexities of the ethnic images held by various groups of people. There were always evaluative components, but in each case, there were both positive and negative responses. It is true that when asked to *rate* their affective attitudes towards Whites, the Black students were strongly and self-consciously negative (see Table 3.2), but their associations reveal a greater ambivalence, although perhaps an ambivalence touched heavily by envy. When they gave, as they did, responses such as *good* to *Whites,* they appeared to be saying: "It is good to be White in America." Few White students in this sample appeared to be totally negative about Blacks, and judging from the pattern of responses, few were totally free of stereotyped prejudices about Blacks.

A Basic Principle of Image Projection: Contrast

An important general principle is illustrated by both the comparative study of national images and the data on race and ethnicity among students in Washington, D.C. It is that the images we project on other people are made up chiefly of those components that easily contrast with our perceived characteristics of ourselves. There is an active seeking of contrast or opposition. Thus, physical characteristics are an important component of the Korean image of *Americans. Large noses* and *big-boned* are notable characteristics of *Americans*. These contrast with Korean self-image, though only implicitly, for they seldom use the opposites to describe themselves, a general feature of such contrastive thinking. The contrasts with *Japan,* concentrate upon mental characteristics. It is the case, however, that the Japanese are *short* in the eyes of the Koreans, and although we would not be so aware of a difference in the average heights between Japanese and Koreans, there is one.

Overwhelmingly, the image that the White and Spanish-speaking students have of Blacks is tied up with the single contrast *Black–White*. For the Black students, the contrast is more detailed. It has to do with the myriad of ways in which they perceive their lives as being different from those of White Americans. It is reasonable to suppose that it is easier to sustain an insensitive prejudice when the contrasts are simpler and focused upon abstractions, such as Blackness or Whiteness, than when the contrasts come from more or less concrete traits and actions, whether real or imagined. To the extent that there was a "reverse racism" among the Black students, it was fundamentally of a different character than was the racism of the White students, and, we must say, of the Spanish-speaking students.

The disposition of human beings to think in contrasts or opposites is well known (Deese, 1965; Greenberg, 1966; Lyons, 1963; Ogden, 1932). The mental act of contrast is something of a primitive in human thinking. It is, evidently, a universal characteristic, for Greenberg (1966) pointed out that pairing of adjectives into opposites is universal among languages. It undoubtedly has a simple perceptual parallel in the incompatibility of certain attribute states. A thing cannot be both hot and cold in the same place, or good and bad in exactly the same characteristic. Whatever the reason, it creates difficulty when we attempt to give logical accounts of human thinking. Logic, of course, is easily thought of as being reduced to a kind of binary primitive categorization of its own. Yes–no, inclusion–exclusion, on–off, true–false, are, of course, all binary categories. However, there is a fundamental and important difference between the operations upon the binary states of a logic and the binary state of opposition. The logical binary expresses the relation between a set and its complement. In a two-valued logic, all things that are not true are false. The complement of an existential set, x is not $-x$, an infinite set. The "not" of oppositional logic, however, is not necessarily an infinite set, and it is, furthermore, ambiguous. The opposite of x is not necessarily the infinite set of everything that is not x in the particular domain under consideration; it may be something specific, such as y. This is clearly so for contradictory opposites, but it tends also to be so even for the so-called contraries. A not-so-tender chicken is probably tough. An unfriendly act is not just an act that is not friendly (in the neutral sense), it is not friendly in the very specific sense of being an act of enmity.

Furthermore, as is well known by now (Deese, 1973), the negation of an opposite tends to be itself negatively evaluated, even when the negation is not overtly marked. Thus, not only is *unfriendly* negative in evaluation, but *bad* or *fat* (the opposites of *good* and *thin*) are also. An author who describes his heroine as "not beautiful" runs the risk of having his readers think her to be ugly, when perhaps all he means is that "she is neither beautiful nor ugly."

The Black students are, judging from the data we have reviewed here, less likely to think about their own ethnicity and that of others in terms of simple oppositional dichotomies, with all their ambiguity, negative affect, and potential for oversimplification. That the Spanish-American students do tend to think this way indicates that they probably accept the implied dichotomy and, in so doing, think of themselves as *White*. Whether a Puerto Rican sample would do so is another matter. For the Chicano culture of the Southwest, there may be another opposite--*Anglo–Chicano* or *White–La Raza*. Wherever they are in contact with a sizable Black community, there is the potential for the three-way opposition, *Black–White, Black–Chicano,* and *Anglo–Chicano.* In general, wherever we encounter very high response scores settling on a particular word, we may suspect some oversimplified view of the concept in question. Opposition is not the only simplifying schema for our thinking, but in a very large number of cases, whenever we find a very high response score, we might expect to find an opposition implied. The highest response scores in the Washington, D.C. data were *Blacks* to *Whites* and *Whites* to *Blacks* given by the Spanish speaking and White students, respectively.

This last point reminds us that the often-encountered tendency of words to yield opposites in free association was responsible for many psychologists failing to see that free associations yielded meaningful relations in subjective experience. Everyone recognizes that *good* is not similar to *bad,* it is the opposite. But as was pointed out more than 10 years ago (Deese, 1965; McNeill, 1966), what opposites in word association tell us is that our subjects are aware of the fact that the words in question are binary states of the same semantic feature. In Chapter 1, we pointed out that *slavery* as a response to *freedom* has a deeper significance for Black respondents than for White respondents. A semantic feature given by the binary contrast *slavery–freedom* is most salient in the subjective world of Black Americans.

The oppositional schema, of course, does not exhaust the list of structures by which we attempt to simplify our understanding of the world. We shall encounter others in later chapters, where particular confluences of groups and concepts reveal them.

4 Images of the Social Environment

The notion of image, in the sense used in the preceding chapter, has a simple and natural extension to all concepts that are important to more or less homogeneous groups of individuals. In addition to images of such significant abstractions as nation and race, we all carry images of our social environment. More than just the familiar patterns of streets and buildings, our city or neighborhood is a place with characteristics that are perceptual and at the same time evaluative, cognitive, and emotional. Moreover, these more or less well-defined physical entities, cities, neighborhoods, and the like have names, and these names, in their own right, become invested with psychological meaning. Furthermore, there are social abstractions, such as work or boss, that provide equally important components of our environment.

In Chapter 5 we cover the differences between what might be called *perceptual images* and *linguistic images*. But because linguistic images are, in a sense, ubiquitous in a way in which our direct perceptions cannot be, we deal, in this more general context, with the linguistic images. Furthermore, we rarely deal with the physical realities of our environment, rather we cope with some abstract, linguistically represented aspect of it.

Our social environment is, of course, more than the natural and artifactual surroundings. It encompasses the people, the institutions around us, and the quality of our relations with them. It also encompasses certain significant nonphysical abstractions such as mental illness. We live in a society in which the concept *mental illness* plays a central role. The existence of that concept and the way it is understood makes the social environment for middle-class Americans unique in some specifiable way. One of the functions of associative data and associative group analysis is to specify those properties of such significant concepts that make certain features of the social environment salient for various groups of people. It is not our purpose here to present a detailed analysis of the cognitive structures of some particular social group or to make particular social comparisons, but rather to illustrate the richness of associative data in providing insights into cognitive structures that determine the social environment.

In this chapter we present data concerned with (a) a comparison of Black, White, and Spanish-speaking residents of Washington, D.C.; (b) a characterization of self-perception in the social milieu of Black and White college students; (c) a study of the interpersonal relations and cultural adaptation of Filipinos serving in the United States Navy;[1] and (d) a brief account of the perception of residents of a portion of the United States about the rest of the country. The first comparison deals largely with problem areas (e.g., mental illness and drug addiction), the second, with an attempt to capture the total social environment; the third, with acculturation; and the fourth, with locale.

A COMPARATIVE STUDY OF SOCIAL MILIEU

Data Collection

The Black, White, and Spanish-speaking samples each contained 156 persons. That enabled analyses to be performed on subsamples of at least 26 individuals. The samples were evenly divided by sex, and they were divided into three income levels, representative of the highest, lowest, and middle quintiles of income in the D.C. Metropolitan area in the 1970 census. Two age ranges were sampled: a young group, from 18 to 20, and a middle-aged group, from 40 to 50. The samples for all three ethnic groups were comparable in education, marital status, etc.

The Spanish-speaking individuals were tested in Spanish. Very close lexical translations of the stimulus words is possible between Spanish and English, but, as we pointed out earlier, the psychological meanings of easily translatable words may be very different. Because the Spanish responses are in a different language, we cannot, in these observations, dissociate language and other aspects of culture. In the next chapter, however, we examine some data in which the same responses are obtained from the same groups in two languages.

Finally, we should once again remind the reader that a sample of Spanish-speaking persons in Washington, D.C., even if the majority are Spanish Americans, is apt to be very different from a sample obtained, for example, in

---

[1] The term *Filipino* is, strictly speaking, a linguistic one describing the major and official language of the Philippine Republic. Despite a certain confusion, both because of the ethnic –linguistic issue (Spanish as well as various non-Filipino Tagalog languages coexist in the Philippine Republic) and the spelling issue, we have retained the name Filipino.

the Southwest or in New York. Suffice it to say that the majority of our sample consisted either of naturalized Americans or persons in the process of being naturalized and whose countries of origin were, for the most part, in Central and South America.

The Data

Table 4.1 compares the responses to *mental health* from the White sample with those from the Spanish-speaking sample. First of all, it is apparent that the constellation *sick—treatment—help* was far more salient for the Anglo sample than for the Spanish sample. This is despite the fact that the constellation *doctor—hospital* was about the same for the two groups. On the other hand, the *madness (locura)* group was much stronger for the Spanish-speaking sample than for the Anglo sample. The notion that mental disorders are illnesses had much less importance for the Spanish speakers than for the English speakers. The highest response score for the Spanish speakers was achieved by *loco (crazy)*. The overall correlation between the two distributions was .150, not statistically different from zero.

Our White respondents' view of mental illness as a treatable illness, perhaps involving emotional instability and problems of adjustment, helps explain why White Americans are more likely to take advantage of mental health facilities than are either Blacks or Spanish speakers. Similarly, the Hispanic view, with its emphasis upon madness and little concern with treatment and care suggests that these persons may be the least likely of the three groups to seek treatment. In any event, these possibilities speak to the relevance of such concepts as *mental illness* as being part of the social environment. The example provides an obvious example of the potential utility of associational data in projecting social policy.

On the other hand, the correlation between the distributions to the stimulus *psychiatrist (psiquiatra)*, was .736. The latter figure is more typical of the Anglo—Spanish-speaking correlations in this domain. There are, in the Anglo data, scattered indications of the residue of the notion of *sin* and *shame* connected with mental illness. The responses to *psychiatrist* for both Anglos and Spanish speakers were overwhelmingly positive, although the term *shrink* occurred frequently in the Anglo data, and *bad*, *bullshit*, and *quack* occurred in low numbers in the Anglo data. No equivalent of these occurred in the distributions for the Spanish speakers.

The themes concerned with drugs (*addiction—addicion, marijuana*) showed a curious, large difference in mean response score between the Anglo and Spanish responders. The average score for the concept *addiction* in the Anglo sample was 14.34, whereas it was only 7.13 in the Spanish sample. A similar comparison for *marijuana* yielded 15.97 vs. 10.46, respectively. Evidently, these two concepts were either grossly different in richness of meaning to these two groups or the Spanish group was inhibited in responding. There was a large preponderance of *bad* responses to *marijuana* for the Spanish sample (response score = 495) com-

TABLE 4.1
Response Scores for Concept *Mental Illness* for Anglo and
Spanish-Speaking Samples in Washington, D.C.

Component and Responses	Anglo	Spanish	Component and Responses	Anglo	Spanish
Sick	464	101	Unstable	282	83
Ill, ness	18	52	Unbalance	–	25
Sick	358	–	Sad, ness	99	7
Disease	36	–	Depression	22	10
Pain	13	18	Sorrow	10	–
Brain damage	10	–	Confusion	–	11
Retard, ed	29	10	Lonely	14	–
Treatment	380	108	Lost	14	–
Treat, ment	28	15	Helpless	23	–
Therapy	13	–	Need help	31	–
Cure	41	13	Fear	19	6
Care, ing	18	10	Emotion	10	–
Help	206	29	Nerves (ous)	–	24
Drugs	28	15	Need, s	40	–
Medicine	6	20	Mind	48	41
Study	18	–	Mind	10	–
Teach	10	–	Brain	19	9
Understanding	12	6	Head	19	32
People	74	43	Health	43	41
People	25	–	Health	33	41
Persons	–	28	Mental health	10	–
Friends	10	–	Family	10	16
Society	8	15	Family	–	6
Carter	21	–	Born, birth	10	10
Crazy	140	489	Bad	96	101
Crazy	53	289	Bad	26	50
Madness	–	178	Terrible	10	–
Insane	22	–	Shame	11	–
Schizophrenic	18	–	Sin	14	–
Neurotic (osis)	15	–	Sorry	17	–
Disturbed	20	–	Danger, ous	–	28
Psychotic	12	–	Problem	18	23
Demented	–	12	Miscellaneous	73	38
Fool	–	10	Money	13	12
Doctor	195	232	Poor, poverty	8	15
Doctor	105	65	Good	–	11
Physician	–	12	Have	11	–
Nurse	30	–	Jesus	14	–
Psychologist	8	18	Love	17	–
Psychiatrist	52	138	Common	10	–
Hospital	192	192			
Hospital	146	134			
Institutions	30	–			
Clinic	6	12			
Asylum	–	36			
Sanitorium	10	10			

TABLE 4.2

Mean Correlations between Response Distributions to Selected Domains
for Black, White, and Spanish-Speaking Respondents

Domain and Sample Stimuli	Black/White	White/Spanish	Black/Spanish
Family	.74	.40	.35
(Family, mother, divorce)			
Society	.58	.25	.25
(Society, race, law)			
Sex	.75	.31	.33
(Sex, love, contraception)			
Money	.80	.45	.46
(Money, save, need, rent)			
Education	.72	.27	.29
(Education, college, school)			
Health	.74	.35	.38
(Health, sick, doctor)			
Religion	.71	.46	.43
(Religion, God, church, bible)			
Problems	.57	.23	.19
(War, killing, pollution)			

Note. Means based on Z transformations of original correlations.

pared with the Anglo sample (response score = 259). The response *vice (vicio)*
occurred in the Spanish distribution to *marijuana* with a score of 164 and not at
all in the Anglo distribution. It is possible that strong negative attitudes may have
created inhibitions in the Spanish speakers, but a more plausible reason for the
large difference between Anglos and Spanish speakers is the richer drug-related
vocabulary, particularly slang, possessed by the White respondents.

In general, the Black and White groups resembled one another in their perception of the world more closely than did either the Black and Spanish-speaking
groups or the White and Spanish-speaking groups. This fact is revealed in Table
4.2, which shows the mean correlations for the major domains sampled in this
study. Despite Black and White differences, they share a culture, and this is revealed in the high correlations between their associative responses. These high
correlations between Black and White respondents probably reflect more perception and knowledge than attitudes. Within the domain *society*, for example, the
highest correlation (.84) occurred in the response distributions to the stimulus
word *race*. Whatever their feelings towards one another, Black and White Americans share a central concept of race that is a pervasive part of the American social
environment. Incidentally, the lowest correlation within that domain was to the
concept *freedom* ($r = .23$). When the response distributions to *freedom* are examined, it is apparent that for the Black respondents this concept centered around
the specific situation of Black Americans and their relation to the White majority. For the White respondents, on the other hand, the notion was more abstract

and concerned with political issues and such things as freedom of speech. It is also of interest, in this connection, that the lowest correlations were between White and Black respondents in the highest income bracket. This is evidently the result of a more intellectual critical evaluation of American society by the high-income Black respondents than by the low-income Black respondents. In response to the stimulus word *society*, high-income respondents were more likely to say *bad* or *unfair* than were low-income respondents (response score of 52 compared with 27, respectively).

A COMPARISON OF BLACK AND WHITE STUDENTS

Data Collection

The social milieu in which we live is a complex structure of interrelated institutions, groups, and affiliations. It would be foolish to suppose that we could capture the varieties of subjective understanding of so complex a structure with reactions to a few stimulus words. Nevertheless, it is instructive at this point to show how a generalized picture of a group's understanding of its social milieu can be achieved by combining the response distributions to several stimuli. We have examined how a group of Black and a group of White college students react to 15 stimuli representing such social entities as *family, society,* and *government* and social relations relevant to Black–White interactions such as *equality* and *segregation.* Our purpose in presenting a summary of these data at this point is to illustrate how we may combine the distributions while almost ignoring the specific content of the stimuli. The anchors or points of reference in this analysis are not, then, the stimuli but the groups themselves, namely, White college students (at the University of Maryland) and Black college students (at D.C. Teachers College).

The Data

Table 4.3 lists the major components of the reactions to these stimuli. The percentages, rather than actual response scores, are given because there was a slight difference in the totals for the two groups (9,945 for Black students and 10,954 for White students). The table segregates those domains for which the response score totals for the two groups differed by more than one percentage point (approximately 100 in response scores). The largest differences were in *education, jobs,* and *personal improvement,* all of which showed higher scores for the Black students than for the White students. Black scores were also slightly higher for *goals* and *aspirations* as well as for *poverty* and *money.* The impression is that the Black students were *aspiring* and perhaps upwardly mobile. This impression is confirmed by an examination of the individual response scores. *Job, money,*

TABLE 4.3
Percentage of Response Scores to 15 Stimuli Reflecting Social Structure
and Black—White Relations

Higher Scores for Black Students			Higher Scores for White Students		
Response Domain	Black	White	Response Domain	Black	White
Education	9.1	4.6	Government, U.S.	2.2	3.2
Jobs	3.0	1.5	Local government	1.2	2.3
Money	2.5	2.0	United States	1.3	2.4
Poverty	2.5	1.9	Social organizations	0.6	1.3
Environment	1.9	0.7	Ego, individualism	1.9	2.9
Housing	0.8	0.4	Male—Female	1.6	2.3
Goals, aspirations	1.8	1.7	Politics	1.9	2.1
Improvement	1.1	0.5	Sex	0.4	1.1
Blacks	4.5	4.1	Positive evaluation	4.4	4.9
Whites	3.3	1.4	Negative evaluation	5.6	6.3
Civil rights	3.6	2.8	Help, care	1.1	2.0
Violence, crimes	1.7	2.0	Entertainment	1.0	1.5
Religion	5.8	5.1	Achievement	1.3	2.4
Law, norms	1.4	1.2	Consumption, goods	0.9	1.5
War—Peace	1.2	0.6	Health	1.1	1.2
			Communicating	1.0	1.5
			Freedom, independence	1.6	3.0
			Equality, fairness	2.3	2.8
			Social problems	1.4	2.0
			Racism	1.9	2.0

compensation, and employment were all responses with much higher scores for Black than for White students. The only responses that were obviously higher for White than for Black students in this domain were want, necessary, and need.

The Black students were also more conscious of where they lived. Housing, ghetto, town, urban, and even environment itself were all anywhere from 2 to 10 times higher for Black than for White respondents. The only response with a sizable score on which the two groups were approximately equal was house, and the only response for which the White respondents exceeded the Black respondents was building.

It is not surprising that the Black concern with civil rights exceeded the White concern, but the difference was not a large one. Blacks were more aware of Whites than the White students were themselves, something that is again not surprising, for the Black students were self-consciously aware of themselves as a minority, whereas the White students hardly ever had to think of themselves as distinctly White. Both groups produced the response Blacks, about equally often. The scores for social problems and violence were relatively small and about equal for the two groups.

The White students showed higher response scores in the domains of ego and individualism. The scores were also higher for the White students on responses having to do with *achievement* (*opportunity, business,* etc.) and in responses having to do with *freedom* and *independence.*

Although the sample of stimulus words in this comparison is too small for fine-grained detail and too heavily weighted with concepts having to do with Black—White relations, the data in Table 4.3 show the usefulness of summing response scores across stimuli in assessing some broad important area of life, such as the social environment. In Chapter 8 we return to this matter of establishing response score distributions across broad areas of human concern.

ACCULTURATION IN A SPECIAL SOCIAL MILIEU

We now turn to a more or less detailed account of the study of Filipinos in the United States Navy.[2] That investigation gives us some idea of the usefulness of associative data, not only in establishing the perception of the social environment, but in determining the extent to which cultural adaptation takes place over an extended period of living in a given social environment.

Background

The recruiting of Philippine nationals to serve in the United States Navy has a long history, going back to 1901 and a time when the Philippine Islands were an American possession. Originally limited to service as stewards and preparers of food, Filipinos now serve in 30 different ratings. There are approximately 20,000 Philippine nationals in service in the U.S. Navy as of 1977. They represent the second largest minority group in the Navy. In the interests of promoting racial equality and equal opportunity, the Human Goal Program of the Department of the Navy has been concerned with the roles of Filipinos in the Navy, their relations with their fellow servicemen, and their perception of themselves. As part of that goal, the reactions to Filipino personnel to certain critical concepts were studied using the associative method.

Data Collection

The data for this project were collected in two phases. In the first phase, associative and questionnaire data were obtained from 50 American and 50 Filipino servicemen of comparable age and rating (E-2 to E-9) at Annapolis in December 1975. Associative data from this phase were used to identify critical domains and appropriate themes. In the second phase, associations to 78 concepts representing 14 domains were collected from 150 Americans and 267 Filipinos. The data from this phase provide the major source for the material presented in this

---

[2]These data are reported in greater detail in Szalay, Williams, Bryson, and West, (1976) and Szalay and Bryson, (1977).

chapter. These data were obtained in April and June of 1976 at Norfolk Naval Base, San Diego Naval Base, and the Naval Recruit Training Center in San Diego.

The samples were comparable in age of the respondents and years of service in the Navy. The younger Filipinos were slightly better educated than the younger Americans, and the younger Filipinos were less likely to be married than were the younger Americans. The majority of the Filipinos were Catholic, whereas the majority of the Americans were Protestant. The distributions by pay grade were comparable.

The Data

The response distributions to the concept *Navy* were highly correlated ($r = .818$) for the American and Filipino samples. In detail, the component of *job, career,* or *work* had slightly higher salience for the Americans than for the Filipinos (30% as opposed to 22% of the total response scores); however, the Filipinos were more likely to respond *career* rather than *job* or *work* to *Navy* than were the Americans. The evaluative components were much stronger for the Americans than for the Filipinos (9% to 4% of the total). The distribution of these evaluative components, together with the nature of certain other responses, indicates that the Filipinos were more positive and less ambivalent towards the Navy than were the Americans. The Filipinos also showed a greater awareness of the international aspects and implications of Naval service.

Again, for the concept *job,* the distribution of response scores was virtually identical for the two groups ($r = .871$). Nearly one-quarter of the total response score was given by the one response *work* for both groups. Such a concentration on a single response is unusual in the method of continued association. Evaluative responses for the two groups were about the same (11% of the total for the Americans vs. 10% for the Filipinos), but the negative evaluations were more common for Americans than for the Filipinos. Once again, however, for this concept there were clearly more resemblances than differences between the two groups. A similar pattern held for the concept *pay.*

Not until we come to the concept *advancement* do we begin to detect differences. The correlation between the response score distributions dropped to .570. The major differences were in the components *money* and *opportunity.* *Money* accounted for 23% of the American responses but only 8% of the Filipino responses, whereas *opportunity* accounted for 21% of the Filipino responses but only 11% of the American. The highest single score for the Americans was the response *money*, whereas the highest single score for the Filipinos was *promotion.* The Filipinos seemed to be more aware or concerned about the higher status that goes with advancement than were the Americans.

Despite the traditional role Filipinos have occupied in the U.S. Navy, discrimination is clearly not something that they think of in connection with themselves. The distributions of response scores to the stimulus *discrimination* were once again virtually identical for the two groups ($r = .817$). Both groups thought of discrimination primarily in terms of the *Black–White* polarity. There were only scattered and incidental responses for both groups that might indicate discrimination against Filipinos. The response *Brown* achieved a score of 11[3] for the American sample and 25 for the Filipino sample. The response *Filipinos* achieved a score of 12 for the American sample and 26 for the Filipinos. The response *me* to *discrimination* achieved only a response score of 7 for the Filipinos, whereas such responses as *South, riots,* and *war* all achieved higher scores for the Filipinos.

When we move to the concept *Filipino,* we begin to see some more striking qualitative differences; the correlation between the distributions was still positive, though quite low ($r = .316$). The Americans perceived the Filipinos as being *foreign* (response score of 365), and both the Americans and the Filipinos perceived a problem of language (response score of 201 for Americans and 61 for Filipinos). Even a few Americans were perceptive enough or knew enough about the Filipino language to give the response, *Tagalog.* The highest single response score for the Filipinos was *Brown* (248), although this response was not prominent for the Americans (48). Evaluatively negative responses were relatively small for both groups (57 for Americans and a negligible 22 for Filipinos). The positive response scores were 271 for Americans and 367 for the Filipinos. The highest single response score in the positive category for the Americans was *friendly.* Finally, one component, *bravery,* was respectable in the Filipino responses (5% of the total) but totally absent in the responses of the Americans.

One important point relevant to the topic of the preceding chapter is apparent in the nature of the associative distribution produced by the Americans to *Filipino.* It had no single strong primary response. The highest scoring single response was the neutral one *people.* The absence of a strong primary and the scattering of responses over many responses and domains indicates that the Americans had no strong image of Filipinos as people. In short, they had no clear stereotype(s) to apply to Filipinos. To be sure, something of the original status of Filipinos in the U.S. Navy remains in such responses as *cook* and *steward,* which occurred, though in low frequency. The component *foreign* was strong, so there was an awareness of difference. There was nothing, however, like the powerful *Black–White* contrast or even the clear-cut and well-organized pictures that emerged in response to the names of other East Asian countries – Korea, South Vietnam, or China. The Philippine Islands and Filipinos appear to have largely dropped out of American consciousness.

Much the same pattern emerged for the concept *American.* The correlation between the two distributions was only slightly higher ($r = .466$), and there was evidence, in the responses of the Filipinos, of stereotypic images of Americans.

---

[3]The response scores for the American sample have been multiplied by 1.78 to compensate for the difference in sample size (150 to 267).

The typical East Asian physical responses to *American* emerged (*tall,* etc.). Positive response scores (141) outnumbered negative ones (26). As in the responses to *Filipino,* there was, on the part of the Filipinos, a concern with *language.* There was no evidence for an *American—Filipino* contrast or a *White—Brown* contrast.

A very clear picture of cultural differences emerges when we consider the conceptions that Filipinos and Americans had of *interpersonal relations.* This concept was presented to the Filipino respondents in Tagalog. The stimulus used for them was *pakisama,* the Filipino word that elicits a broadly defined Tagalog concept as close as possible to the notion of *interpersonal relations.*

There was no similarity between the distribution of responses for the Filipinos and Americans to these concepts ($r = -.004$). To Americans, the concept *interpersonal relations* means first of all *love* and *sex.* Then it is heavily infused with the psychologizing that has become so common in American culture. It is something you *need* and *feel.* However, compared with the Filipino responses, the American responses were scattered, perhaps indicating that the concept lacks the meaningful unity that the notion of *pakisama* has. Ten percent of the total response score for the Americans must be put in a miscellaneous category.

The Filipino concept has a clear central theme. It is *friendship* (probably male). More than one-quarter of the total response score for the Filipinos was given over to the single response *friend.* The idea of *friendship* encompassed 33% of the total. When *neighbors* and *shipmates* were added to this total, it rose to 47% of the total. The response *loyalty* did not occur for the Americans but it did for the Filipinos.

The picture that emerges is clear and strong. There is a central, meaningful structure for the Filipinos. It centers primarily upon male friendships and has a strong component of *cooperation* and *helping.* Finally, it should be noted, the total response score for the Filipinos was one and a half times greater than that for the Americans (after correction for sample size), indicating the high cultural dominance of this concept for Filipinos.

A superficially very different pattern appears to emerge with the concept *friend,* for here the correlation was substantial ($r = .635$). However, the relation of this concept to that of *interpersonal relations* provides a good object lesson in relying too heavily on the overall correlation. As was apparent from the data presented in the last chapter, the correlations within components often differed drastically from the overall correlation (see Table 3.6). For that reason we have presented in Table 4.4 the distributions of responses to *friends.*

There was striking agreement between Americans and Filipinos in such components as *buddies, positive evaluation, people, help,* and *loyalty.* However, a critical difference lies in the component of *pleasure.* There were scattered responses from the Filipino respondents, particularly to the word *happiness,* which has some meaning beyond that of pure pleasure. However, the Americans concentrated upon *fun, party,* and *enjoyment.* As expected, there was certain evi-

TABLE 4.4
Meaning Components and Responses Given to *Friends* by American
and Filipino Enlisted Men in the United States Navy

Components and Responses	Americans	Filipinos	Components and Responses	Americans	Filipinos
Pleasure	395	101	Family	157	32
Party	55	4	Family	43	3
Play	21	9	Relatives	29	10
Fun	190	12	Wife	52	10
Good times	30	16	Home	34	9
Enjoyment	52	5	Navy	88	13
Happy, ness	46	55	Navy	43	–
Need	171	16	Work	45	13
Need, ed	144	16	Negative	123	80
Important	27	–	Bad	16	70
Many–Few	158	65	Enemy	107	10
Many	82	34	Closeness	382	256
Lots	–	11	Forever	22	–
Few	77	15	Close, ness	132	29
Trust	151	105	Intimate	–	15
True	22	19	Sharing	–	13
Trust, worthy	73	40	Together, ness	43	34
Honest	16	11	Understanding	32	87
Respect	–	14	Love, ing	126	78
Loyal	41	10	Positive	230	240
Faithful	–	11	Good	210	221
Buddies	692	490	Best	20	19
Amigo	–	45	People	431	317
Kalbigan (friend)	–	15	People	258	79
Buddy, s	137	81	Man	–	17
Brothers	21	15	Boy, s	12	47
Pal, s	77	46	Women	34	4
Partner, s	–	15	Girl, s	66	73
Company	16	40	Group	–	20
Shipmate	153	76	Americans	–	25
Coworker	20	7	Filipinos	–	22
Companion, ship	101	34	Blacks	25	13
Neighbors	157	97	White, s	14	17
Relation, ship	11	19	Christians	21	–
Help	242	170	Miscellaneous	30	22
Help, er, ing	213	113	Money	–	11
Advice	–	11	Live	11	11
Kind	–	20	Brad	20	–
Nice	28	26			

Note. The American response scores have been multiplied by 1.78 to compensate for the larger Filipino sample.

dence for the semantic polarity *friend–enemy* from the Americans, although very little from the Filipinos. Instead, the Filipinos had a sizable response score associated with *bad*. The concept of a *bad friend* would probably be less strange to a Filipino than to an American. Finally, Americans appeared to *need friends*, whereas the Filipinos did not. These and other features of the resemblances and differences between the two groups to this concept can be seen in Table 4.4.

The responses to the concepts *shipmate* and *commander* were similar for the two groups and contained no surprises. However, the responses to the concept *boss* revealed a subtle difference between Americans and Filipinos and deserve a word of comment. The correlation was moderate ($r = .519$), and there were some interesting differences. Both groups identified the notion with *officers* or *chiefs* and with management responsibilities. But the Filipinos had a stronger component of *superiority* than did the Americans, and they were more likely to attribute *knowledge* to the concept than were the Americans. The negative evaluations were slight in both groups, but the negative response scores for Americans were about three times as high as those for the Filipinos. Both groups identified *boss* with *work* and getting on with the job.

Acculturation

Our samples contained individuals who ranged from being new recruits to being career enlisted men with as much as 25 years of service. Therefore, it is possible to determine the relation between length of service in the Navy and changes in response to critical concepts. In the American sample there were 50 individuals in each of three categories: recruits, those with 1 to 10 years of service and those with 11 to 25 years of service. In the Filipino sample there were 81 recruits and 86 and 100 persons in the other two categories, respectively.

Table 4.5 shows the correlations among these three groups for the American and Filipino samples separately for 14 critical domains. First of all, the correlations were generally, although only slightly, higher for the Americans than for the Filipinos, indicating that there was greater stability, as one might expect, with years of service in the Navy for the Americans than for the Filipinos. However, the correlations were sizable for both the Americans and Filipinos. Three domains for which there was a sizable difference depending upon years of service for the Filipinos were *education, health,* and *recreation.* The recruits were least like those persons with long service on these concepts. On the other hand, the correlations for *religion, work, interpersonal relations,* and *self image* were high and relatively stable. *Recreation, interpersonal relations,* and *friends* were domains in which the American recruits least resembled their seniors.

The correlations between American and Filipino samples for different years of service give clear evidence of acculturation. With the single exception of *interpersonal relations*, the correlations between American recruits and Filipino recruits were lower than were the correlations between the veterans for the two

TABLE 4.5
Correlations among Response Score Distributions to 14 Domains
for American (A) and Filipino (F) Personnel in the U.S. Navy

| Domains | Correlations Within American and Filipino Samples | | | | | | Correlations Between American and Filipino Samples | | |
| | Recruits vs. 1–10 Years | | Recruits vs. 11–25 Years | | 1–10 Years vs. 11–25 Years | | | | |
	A	F	A	F	A	F	Recruits	1–10 Years	11–25 Years
Family	.78	.64	.75	.66	.86	.70	.50	.56	.73
Friends	.65	.58	.57	.61	.69	.65	.42	.41	.61
Society	.61	.63	.65	.73	.68	.74	.39	.42	.53
Sex	.80	.68	.69	.69	.83	.73	.45	.63	.61
Money	.74	.69	.70	.66	.80	.77	.48	.66	.72
Work	.81	.73	.76	.70	.84	.82	.64	.71	.73
Education	.70	.39	.66	.39	.74	.56	.23	.50	.54
Health	.68	.49	.65	.53	.77	.67	.39	.56	.67
Religion	.87	.81	.84	.83	.91	.89	.70	.70	.75
Service	.82	.69	.80	.62	.83	.84	.57	.72	.76
Navy	.77	.65	.68	.65	.84	.80	.59	.66	.79
Recreation	.61	.51	.53	.52	.74	.67	.23	.40	.56
Self image	.67	.70	.58	.69	.68	.79	.38	.54	.57
Interpersonal	.63	.70	.47	.74	.54	.77	.18	.11	.14
Means	.74	.65	.68	.66	.78	.76	.45	.56	.64

Note. All correlations are means based upon Z transformations of six stimuli for each domain.

groups. Some domains, such as *religion* and *work,* were highly correlated to begin with and did not change much with experience, but others, such as *health, recreation, self image, money,* and *sex,* changed greatly. That these changes were the result of the Filipinos becoming more like the Americans is evident when the distributions of response scores are examined.

No better evidence for the nature of the change can be found than the distributions, by years of service, of the Filipinos responding to *Filipino* and *American.* The response scores for the response *White* to *American* declined from an average of 3.30 for the recruits to 2.49 for those with 1 to 10 years service to 1.54 for those with 11 to 25 years of service. The response scores for the response *tall* declined from 1.46 for the recruits to 0 for the other ages. At the same time, phrase-completing or syntagmatic responses, such as *Red Cross* or *Revolution,* increased. The stereotyped picture of *Americans* began to weaken and some of the incidental phrases well known to Americans but likely not to occur to foreigners began to come in. At the same time, the Filipinos' perception of themselves as different began to decline. The response, *Brown,* to Filipino declined from 2.47 for the recruits to 1.92 for those with 1 to 10 years service and 1.30 for those with 11 to 25 years of service. The more nearly universal response *people* replaced *Brown.* There was a small class of responses that indicates sensitivity about language and culture. These increased in response scores from an average of 0.58 for the recruits to 1.37 for those with more than 11 years of service. Other changes reflected more subtle processes. The responses to the stimulus *me* became more Americanized. There was an apparent increase in the emphasis upon the individual, the juxtaposition of *I* and *you,* and a hint of the feeling of loneliness that often appears to characterize the American self-image (Szalay & Maday, 1973).

In summary, the Filipino personnel in the United States Navy take on certain of the perceptions, values, and priorities of the larger social group in the Navy. This process is probably helped by the fact that recruitment into the United States Navy is a voluntary process. It attracts persons who can adjust to a strange culture, and retains those who find the adjustment easy and satisfactory.

SUBJECTIVE GEOGRAPHY

Before concluding this chapter, a brief mention of a study concerned with perception of geographical entities will serve to illustrate another facet of the ability of associative data to capture the perceptions people have to their social environment, as well as the limitations of the discrete associative method compared with the continued method. As part of a project (unpublished) on the perception students at the University of South Dakota have of their native state, Hilda Wing[4] obtained associations from these students by a modified method of discrete association to the names of all 50 states. Because these data were gathered for another purpose, they do not lend themselves to the kind of detailed treatment we have given other data, but they are sufficiently interesting to warrant some discussion.

First of all, these North Dakota students had a highly stereotyped and negative attitude towards most of the Southeastern states. *Poverty* and *racial conflict* were frequent components for *Alabama, Arkansas, Florida, Georgia, Louisiana, Mississippi,* and *South Carolina.* Most of these states were also *hot* and *humid. Violence, swamps, storms,* and *prejudice* occurred as frequent responses to two or more of these Southern states. However, it is interesting and important to notice that certain states of the old Confederacy were excluded from this unpleasant portrayal. Florida was said to be *warm* more often than *hot,* and *beaches, oranges, sunshine* and *sports* all gave a more positive cast. *North Carolina, Virginia, Tennessee,* and *Texas* also appeared to be exempted from the general stereotype of the South. *Virginia* was perceived in terms of *beautiful hills, history,* and *accent,* whereas *North Carolina* elicited *hills, hilly green, mountains,* and *seaboard. Texas,* of course, was overwhelmingly *large* or *big,*

---

[4]These data were kindly supplied to J. Deese by Dr. Wing.

and *Tennessee* was characterized by *Blue Ridge Mountains* (sic), *hilly,* and *plateau.*

Eastern industrial states such as *Connecticut, Delaware, New Jersey,* and *New York* were *crowded, hemmed in,* and *polluted.* Once again, there were exceptions to the generally negative connotations. *Massachusetts* was pleasantly perceived as was *Pennsylvania.* The Western states were generally favorably perceived, most of all *Colorado.* Also, these students seemed to know more about *Colorado* than any other state except their own and its immediate neighbors.

It is only when there are enough stimuli within a domain that patterns, such as the exclusion of certain states from the stereotypes about the South, emerge. However, the many sets of associative data now generally available, largely using the method of discrete association, enable us to detect images of the social environment here and there. Unfortunately, most published norms contain generalities such as *country, ocean,* or *home* rather than *Israel, Pacific Ocean,* or *my home.* An exception are the norms provided by Marshall and Cofer (1970). Because of their interest in the Bousfield category norms, they tabulated free associations to the names of 16 countries. We did not describe these data in the previous chapter because they offered so little that could be described as novel information. They told us that *Germany,* when the norms were collected in 1961, was still tainted with the *Nazi* era and of all the nations sampled, still had the most *warlike* image. Also, *Korea,* 8 years after the war in that country was over, still evoked a strong memory of *war* in the minds of the New York University college students tested.

Our main point in evoking these data at this point is to make apparent the great advantage of the method of continued association compared with that of discrete association for determining the structure of subjective meaning. For the 16 countries to which Marshall and Cofer's (1970) sample responded, a total of 21% of all responses to the names of the 16 countries consisted of the response *country.* This was in the context, of course, of other concepts as stimuli. The only cases in which *country* was not an overwhelming primary were: *Cuba, Castro; Korea, war; Mexico, Spain; Portugal, Spain.* Whatever Spain's national fortunes in the past two centuries, it still apparently serves as a symbol for a whole culture.

The point is, however, that the uninteresting response *country* dominates the distributions, squeezing out responses that might be more revealing. If the method of continued association had been used, other responses would necessarily have occurred in much higher frequency, and there would have been more of them. Thus, however interesting the data obtained in Wing's survey, they would have been richer if some variant of the method of continued association had been used, instead of a variant of the method of discrete association. This tendency of the distributions obtained by the method of discrete associations to be strongly dominated by a single response or by a small number of responses makes the large reservoir of data collected by this method (e.g., Postman & Keppel, 1970) less interesting than they might otherwise be.

5 Association in Various Modes

In the past several chapters we have reviewed evidence to show that associative distributions offer useful information about cultural meaning and that they are particularly sensitive to the perceptual and affective components of meaning. A basic part of a particular cultural frame of reference is the language of that culture. In this chapter we focus attention upon the influence of language upon word associations. A particular question addressed here is whether or not two culturally different groups give different patterns of associations because of the different languages they speak or because of different cultural milieus. One way to examine this question is to compare the word associations of people who speak two different languages.

BILINGUAL ASSOCIATIONS

The Background

There is, it turns out, a modest literature on associations given in two different languages by bilinguals. The best-known investigation, perhaps, is that by Kolers (1963), in which he studied associations in English to English stimuli, associations in a speaker's native language to English stimuli, native words as responses to native stimuli, and English responses to native stimuli. The native languages were German, Spanish, and Thai. All testing was in a single session. Although stimuli were repeated in both the native and English languages, Kolers treated the data as discrete associations. His main result was that only about one third of the responses in one language translated those in the other. This disappointingly small proportion was not influenced by whether the associations were interlingual or intralingual. He noted that words referring to concrete, manipulatable objects were more likely to be the same than words referring to abstract states or emotions. He took his data to indicate that experiences and memories are not stored in some supralinguistic form but are tagged and stored separately in the language appropriate to the experience in question.

Dalrymple-Alford and Aamiry (1970) achieved much the same result in a study employing English—Arabic bilinguals. Their proportion of translatable responses, 28%, was only slightly smaller than that found by Kolers. However, Dalrymple-Alford and Aamiry were more sensitive to the content of words and rejected Kolers' notion of separate semantic storage in favor of the view that exact translations of stimuli simply are not possible. They pointed out, for example, that the equivalent Arabic word for *doctor* would never be used to refer to a holder of a doctoral degree who is not a medical practitioner. They also pointed to the importance of connotative features in determining associations (the stubborness of mules, wisdom of owls, etc.). Therefore, Dalrymple-Alford and Aamiry argued, the differences in associations given to translation pairs reflect differences in the meaning of the stimulus words. Further, it might be pointed out that Taylor (1971) was able to show that accomplished bilinguals (in French and English) switch back and forth between languages easily in continuous association. Such a result argues for language-interdependent processing.

One of the problems with these studies as well as with others (e.g., Shugar & Gepner-Wiecko, 1971) is that the stimuli were not selected for culturally relevant reasons. Often, they were selections from the Kent-Rosanoff list or were selected to represent grammatical categories or concrete vs. abstract concepts, etc. Furthermore, the method of discrete associations was used, a method that tends to produce low test—retest correlations (Brotsky & Linton, 1967; Gegoski & Riegel, 1967) compared with the method of continued associations. Therefore, before reaching any conclusions about the specificity of associations to a particular language, we need to examine data from culturally relevant stimuli obtained by the method of continued association.

A Linguistic-Cultural Comparison

Such data are provided by an investigation employing Korean and Colombian students residing in the Washington, D.C. area (Szalay & Windle, 1968). The samples contained 50 bilingual Korean students and 50 bilingual Colombian students. Both samples contained equal numbers of both sexes. These samples were tested 1 week apart, first in the respondent's native language and then in English. For additional comparisons and in order to provide a benchmark for test—retest reliability, data from monolingual American students in the Washington area are presented in the following discussion.

Some general features of the data need to be mentioned before we present the relevant cross-linguistic comparisons. First of all, the Koreans produced fewer responses in their native language than did the other two groups. This is probably the result of the use of the Korean alphabet, which is more difficult and time-consuming to write than is the Roman alphabet. Usually, when responding in a secondary language, people produce many fewer responses, but because of the greater ease of writing, the Korean subjects produced almost as many responses in English as they did in Korean. In contrast, the Colombian group produced noticeably fewer responses in English than in Spanish. The Colombian group had a more limited vocabulary and less fluency in English than did the Koreans. This is consistent with the fact that they had a shorter history of residence in the United States; the Koreans, on the average, had been in the United States for more than 2.5 years, whereas the Colombians had, on the average, less than a year of residence. Because the Colombian group showed less proficiency in English, the main analyses of the data concentrated on the Korean responses.

Table 5.1 shows the identical or translation—equivalent associations for Koreans responding in Korean and English and expressed as a percentage of all associations. These percentages are analogous to the affinity measure described in Chapter 2.

The results, on the whole, show more agreement between languages than similar comparisons using the method of discrete associations. This is not surprising, since the test-retest reliability of data obtained by the method of continued associations and weighted according to the scheme outlined in Chapter 2 is much higher than that for discrete associations. It can, as we noted in that chapter, ex-

TABLE 5.1

Associative Affinity across Languages to the Same Words with Data on
Test—Retest Comparisons in the Same Language

Words	Comparison Between Native Language and English		Reliability Estimates Based on Monolingual English Sample		
	Korean	Colombian	Test—Retest[a]	Test—Retest[b]	Split-half
Hungry	44.6	35.8	61.2	56.8	55.2
Poor	34.7	44.0	54.2	49.0	50.2
Food	42.5	43.4	59.0	51.6	56.6
Rice	36.2	44.4	68.6	58.7	67.2
Money	42.5	44.7	56.4	50.2	58.4
Beggar	43.4	47.8	59.6	53.2	58.6
Ancestors	44.4	33.0	47.2	46.2	53.3
Social	25.0	40.4	—	45.4	55.4
Equality	31.6	34.4	—	50.8	53.4
Socialism	38.2	50.1	—	47.5	56.0
Mean	38.3	41.8	58.0	50.9	56.4
Standard deviation	6.1	5.5	6.1	4.1	4.3

Note. Data are percentages of overlapping responses.
[a]One month.
[b]One year.

ceed .90. The data for American samples are percentages affinity based upon responses to identical stimuli at different times or upon a split of the sample into two groups of subjects. Although the agreement between languages was higher than by the method of discrete associations, it was smaller than between repeated stimuli in the same language, as evidenced by the data from the various American samples tested in English.

It is less this kind of general difference that is of interest than the relation between the linguistic differences and the cultural differences. A comparison of Koreans responding in Korean with Koreans responding in English reveals how the particular language employed affects the associations. A comparison of Koreans responding in English with Americans responding in English reveals the combined effects of culture and language upon associations. Finally, a split-half comparison of an American sample provides a baseline to evaluate the interlingual and intercultural comparisons.

Correlations between affinity indices across and within languages and cultures reveal a strong commonality but an interesting pattern of differences. A split-half correlation of affinity relations for the American responders in English was .97. The correlation drops to .84 when we compare Korean responders in Korean and Korean responders in English. The correlation drops further to .78 when we compare American responders in English and Korean responders in English. Finally, the correlationn drops to .72 when we compare Korean responders in Korean and American responders in English--a result of the combined influences of language and culture. These correlations are based upon samples that vary from 94 to 45 word pairs, so they are stable.

Two Examples of Cultural Differences

If we examine the total distributions to the concept *hungry* in Table 5.2, a more subtle but important matter emerges. In English, responses were heavily concerned with American conceptions associated with *food*. Such responses comprised 154 or 29.7% of the total. In Korean, these responses accounted for only 94 or 18.5% of the total. Instead, the responses in Korean centered on those features that so often are uppermost in the minds of persons from the third world — misery. Such responses as *pitiful, orphan, poverty,* and *war* accounted for a total of 179 or 35.2% of the total. In short, when changing from Korean to English as the mode of response, these two components reversed in degree of salience.

Much the same pattern exists with the more abstract concept *equality*. Table 5.3 lists the responses given in Korean and English to this word. The salience as well as specific responses changed. For example, in Korean there was a larger component dealing with abstract political issues (*democracy, communism, peace,* etc.), achieving a response score of 155 or 32.7% of the total in Korean and 192 or 57.8% of the total in English. The comparable figures for responses centering

TABLE 5.2
Response Scores for Responses Given to the Stimulus
Hungry in Korean and in English

Response	Response Scores	
	Korean	*English*
Cooked rice	107	6
People, person	35	6
Pitiful	27	–
Orphan	22	3
Poverty	46	32
War	26	13
Time	12	–
Meat	11	–
Child	10	–
Sympathy	10	–
Life	10	–
Must eat	10	–
Poor people	10	–
Pain, ful	10	20
Struggle	–	12
Hunger	12	26
Restaurant	7	19
Bread	8	23
Drink	3	24
Money	40	72
Poor	28	75
Eat	13	63
Food	51	125
Totals	508	519

on *civil rights* and *equality* of *opportunity* were 74 or 15.6% of the total in Korean and 93 or 28.0% of the total in English. For the remaining large component of this distribution, *people*, the figures were 155 or 32.7% of the total for Korean and 33 or 9.9% of the total in English.

In general, associating in Korean leads Koreans to think of issues and problems characteristic of their Korean social environment. Thus, *equality*, in their native language, leads them to think of equality of the sexes, something that is an issue in Korean culture. The English word equality, on the other hand, reminds them of racial equality, an aspect of the concept brought to their attention by exposure to the racial problems endemic in their host nation.

For these two concepts, *hunger* and *equality*, there is a difference in the salience of components of meaning, depending upon which language is used. The differences do not so much reflect differences in the languages themselves, considered as abstract linguistic entities, as much as differences in cultural

TABLE 5.3
Response Scores for Responses Given to the Stimulus
Equality in Korean and in English

Response	Response Scores	
	Korean	*English*
Men and women	92	14
Equality	67	21
Democracy	107	78
Friend	27	3
Power	23	0
Communism	27	5
Human being	23	3
Equality of men and women	35	18
Personality	13	0
Education	15	3
Peace	20	9
Position	19	9
Opportunity	0	10
Job	0	10
Segregation	3	14
Law	6	18
People	0	13
Negro	1	14
Good thing	0	14
Civil rights	1	15
Freedom	14	35
Human right	0	26

experiences. Koreans appear to think differently about the notion *equality* in English than they do in Korean not because the languages differ but because the use of one or another language causes them to think about concepts and issues important in the culture of that language. In the lexical sense, the meaning of *equality* in Korean and English may not be all that different, but in terms of the subjective experience of Koreans in two cultures, the subjective meaning of the concept may be very different for them in Korean and English.

While there are differences associated with language, there are also similarities. Lambert, Havelka and Crosby (1958) note that bilinguals with experiences in separated language acquisition show comparatively greater semantic differences than bilinguals with experience in what they call "fused acquisition contexts." The data reported above were from subjects who mostly learned English in the United States and thus belong to the category described by Lambert, Havelka and Crosby as "separated language acquisition."

Implications

The above findings have two main implications. They suggest that the distributions of word associations primarily reflect cultural experience. Secondly, because bilinguals produce different associations when using different languages does not justify the conclusion that these are linguistically determined differences. We hasten to add that linguistically determined differences are quite possible. A little noted but important effect observed by Shugar and Gepner-Wiecko (1971) makes this point. Their comparisons of bilingual Polish-English speakers is in complete agreement with the data reported above, but they also point out that certain lexical and morphological characteristics of a language can have direct effects upon word associations. Polish is a highly inflected language, and case or gender endings influence the nature of associative responses in Polish. For example, the word *ciemny* (*dark* in its masculine form) tends to elicit only nouns with masculine endings or other adjectives in the masculine gender. Reasonable responses in the wrong gender like *noc* (*night*) simply do not occur. Similarly, concepts which are specific to a particular language (*l'espirit* or *Weltanschaung*) are likely to produce language specific associations as well.

While word associations occur in the context of lexical meaning, of course, it is cultural experience that produces the unique distribution of associations to particular words in a particular language. Because of the close relation between associative distributions and cultural experience, the degree of associative similarity between a word in one language and its translation in another provides an index of the extent to which the translation has captured the spirit of the original. Associations reveal nuances that might otherwise be detected only by someone who was intimately acquainted with both languages and cultures.

PICTURES AS ASSOCIATIVE STIMULI

Associative stimuli need not be verbal, nor indeed is it necessary that the responses be so. Although nonverbal ways of characterizing associative stimuli are difficult to arrange, it is not an impossible task. Karwoski, Odbert, and Osgood (1942) had subjects draw pictures as associative responses to each of a series of simple sounds produced by a clarinet. A typical response, for example, to a single tone that first increased in loudness and then grew softer was a line that became thicker in the middle or rose on the page and then fell. In short, as with verbal associations, some significant property of the stimulus is reflected in the response. Although nonverbal interpretations of things are interesting, useful, and perhaps of aesthetic significance, they have serious limitations. The importance of language is revealed in the difficulty we have interpreting nonverbal responses and in the great diversity of responses to even very simple and highly structured stimuli.

Thus, for our purposes, nonlinguistic responses to nonlinguistic (or linguistic) stimuli must remain an oddity of sorts. However, verbal or linguistic responses to stimuli that are not in language are important. It is possible to compare an object or pictorial representation of an object with the name of the object. It is not surprising that there is a large literature on associations to nonverbal stimuli and on a comparison of nonverbal stimuli with verbal stimuli.

Differences Between Words and Pictures

As with the literature on bilingual associations, there is a strong tendency in that literature to emphasize the differences in associative responses between pictures and words. For example, Deno, Johnson, and Jenkins (1968) said, "the results of the present study clearly show that the associative meanings for words and pictures which elicit a common label are dissimilar" (p. 284). Yet, the data upon which that assertion rests reveal that for the 40 words and comparable pictures they used, the average picture–word overlap in specific responses was 56.5%. It is true that an appreciable proportion of that overlap was the result of the subjects responding to the pictures by a label. A label may be regarded as a kind of supraordinate response to a picture. When we see the word *chair,* we do not overtly respond with *chair,* although as Bousfield, Whitmarsh, and Danick (1958) and Deese (1965) have insisted, we must represent the visual display of the word to ourselves in some way or other; whether the representation is phonetic or not is a matter of dispute (see Rozin & Gleitman, 1977). We may respond with *furniture* or some other word representing a supraordinate class. When we see a picture of a chair, however, we know that it is a specific instance of a class of things that have the label chair, and so we feel free to name that class. In fact, we must regard the label as a response of identification; therefore, if the picture does not elicit the word we regard as corresponding to the picture from a fair number of respondents, the picture and the word can be regarded as only weakly corresponding.

Words have components of meaning, and by choosing to give particular associations to those words, we indicate what components of meaning have been aroused by the word. But we seldom respond to part of a word (an exception may be in klang associates); we treat the word as whole. We may, however, respond to just a part of a complex picture. We may, in fact, label just a portion of a picture. The picture of a well-known person, *Martin Luther King* for example, may well elicit the word *mustache,* a label for a portion of the picture. Some of these details of the relations between pictures and words in association demand more exploration than they have received, and, therefore, we shall present the results of a study that do not bear on our major concern – the interpretation of culture through associations – but which provide a general background for the relations between pictures and words.

A Comparison of Words and Pictures Using Associative Group Analysis

This study made use of 50 University of Maryland undergraduates as subjects. These subjects were asked to associate to both words and pictures. Some of the words and pictures were very simple, such as *line* or *triangle*. Others represented well-known objects, such as *tree, forest,* or *girl*. Still others represented abstractions of actions and relations, such as *buy, fight,* or *hostility*. Some of the linguistic stimuli consisted of noun phrases, such as *a white horse* or *a proud person,* whereas still others were verb phrases, such as *to buy a house* or *to fight a person*. There were pictures, line drawings by a skilled artist, to correspond to each of these.

Surprisingly, the average inter subject agreement appeared to be higher for pictures than for words (inter subject agreement was determined by correlations between randomly split-halves of the subject sample). There was, however, great individual variability from stimulus to stimulus. The verb *buy* produced a reliability correlation of .93, whereas the noun *friendship* produced a correlation of .21. The picture representing the verb phrase *to fight a person* produced a correlation of .92, whereas the lowest pictorial correlation (.44) was to the picture representing the concept *people*.

The words produced, on the average, higher dominance scores than did the pictures, and the pictures were also more variable in their dominance scores than were the words, though dominance scores to the phrases were low and variable. That some pictures were much inferior to the words in their ability to elicit meaningful responses is not surprising in view of the need for subjects to scan pictures for details. In general, the correspondence between pictures and words was surprisingly good, even for certain of the abstract words and phrases. One of the "simple" stimuli, *stone,* produced a poor correspondence between picture and word. The highest response score for an identifying response to the picture of the *stone* was *circle*. Other high identifying response scores for this picture were *egg, potato, oval,* and *hole*. Evidently, it was not a good representation for the concept *stone*. Other examples in which the principal identifying responses indicated misinterpretation included *people (walking), to buy a house (mortgage),* and *to help a girl (father)*.

The similarity between the response distributions to pictures and words and word phrases was, on the average, higher than we might have expected, given the tenor of the conclusions drawn by those who have studied the correspondence between associations and words by the method of discrete association. The average correlation between picture and word distributions after a Z transformation was .68. There were, of course, wide variations. The highest were for words exhibiting high reliability in both modes; concepts such as *forest, run,* and *groups* all had correlations above .80. The lowest, not surprisingly, was for *stone,* .14, for which, of course, the pictorial representation was often misunderstood.

Finally, a content analysis of the distribution of responses scores as a whole to pictures and words yielded certain clear, stable differences. It is not surprising that abstract concepts (e.g., *aggression, ego, violence,* and *me*) and traits of character (e.g., *mad, strong,* and *good*) occurred more often to words than to pictures, whereas facial expressions (e.g., *frown, smile*) and activities (e.g., *fight, move, run*) occurred more often to pictures. There were exceptions, however. *Happy* occurred more often to pictures than to words, as did *anger.*

Although these data are limited by the small number of concepts investigated (35) they present, we believe, a more accurate account of the relation between verbal and pictorial representation and associative meaning than do any of the investigations utilizing the method of discrete association. They show us that the response distributions for words and corresponding pictures can be highly correlated — as is the case with the relation between responses distributions to the same word in two different languages. They also show us that extremely low correlations between pictorial representations and words is likely to be due to misinterpretations of the pictorial representation. Pictures induce greater salience of concrete as opposed to abstract components. Pictures, in general, produce lower dominance scores than do words and verbal phrases. This is likely due to the tendency of people to search pictures for details to which to respond. There is evidence that people do respond to the specific details of pictures. For example, the picture of *house* had a driveway prominent in it. *Driveway* achieved a response score of 58 for the pictorial representation and 0 for the word. There is a natural tendency to produce responses based on visual impressions. Finally, pictures produce at least as reliable response score distributions as those to words and word phrases. With this much background in the general nature of the picture—word relation, we can turn to an account of these as stimuli in the investigation of culturally significant concerns.

Culturally Relevant Comparison of Pictures and Words

A study of Black and White students provides our data. The 50 Black students came from District of Colombia Teachers College; the 50 White students, from the University of Maryland. There were eight words used as stimuli (*me, friends, family, student, Blacks, Whites, Society,* and *I*) and 30 pictures. Ten pictures came from the Thematic Apperception Test (TAT) and the remaining 20 came from magazines (e.g., *Ebony*); they all represented social interactions between Blacks and Whites. For our purposes here, the major emphasis is the use of pictures of stimuli.

There has been a fair amount of concern on the part of those interested in the clinical use of the TAT to provide pictures with which particular racial groups can identify. There exists, for example, a version of the TAT for Blacks (Thompson, 1949). It is interesting to note that although there were Black—White differences in associative responses to the 10 TAT pictures (depicting White persons interacting) the Black–White correlations were sizable and enormously higher than the typical reliability coefficients achieved for the standard scoring of the TAT. They ranged from .81 to .38, with a mean (after Z transformation) of .63. The average split–half correlation for all 30 pictures used in this study was .85. The pictures with the two lowest correlations were ambiguous, particularly with respect to expression of affection or conflict.

The distribution of responses produced by Black and White subjects shows that there were few responses unique to one or the other group. Rather, as before, the chief difference was in the dominance or salience of particular components. An exception may be the responses *fear, afraid,* and *frighten*, which appeared in the Black distributions but not in the White distributions to the first picture. To the fourth picture the White respondents achieved higher scores on the components *tender* and *touch* than did the Blacks, whereas the Blacks achieved higher scores on words (*affection, love*) expressing the abstract relation of *love*. When the distributions as a whole are examined, the strong impression is of such linguistic or cognitive differences rather than a difference in the affect, feeling, motivations, and emotions tapped in the two groups by the pictures.

If we take the point of view that the TAT pictures are meant to capture various aspects of the affective nature of human interactions, it may be worthwhile to consider the pictures as a whole rather than individually. An examination of the response scores for particular responses totaled across all pictures shows some differences, but once again, differences that are mainly cognitive or in a mode of expression rather than in qualitatively different perceptions of human relations and interactions as depicted in the pictures. For example, as we have already noted, Blacks tended to respond more with the word *love* than did Whites, but the difference for all words expressing positive human relations was not particularly striking (863 for Blacks and 701 for Whites). In the *death* category, Blacks were far more likely than Whites to respond with *murder* and *kill* (response score of 136 compared with 29), whereas Whites had a slightly greater tendency to respond with the abstract term *death* itself (194 for Blacks, 263 for Whites).

In addition to the 10 TAT pictures, data were obtained on 20 pictures, photographs taken from magazines, showing social interactions between Blacks and Whites. For 4 of these, the picture showing the interaction was shown first, followed by pictures of the individual participants separately. The Black–White correlations for all pictures ranged from .26 (significant at the .05 level) to .91, so, as in the case of the TAT pictures, there was both high agreement between Blacks and Whites and some differences.

Two examples will illustrate the nature of the differences between Blacks and Whites. These differences are more interesting than those for the TAT pictures, but there are also similarities. In one picture, a younger White woman is shown in conversation with an older Black woman. The White woman is in the foreground and appears to be talking rather vigorously to the Black woman, who is listening attentively. The White respondents perceived this relationship as being *friendly* (response score of 90), whereas the Blacks did only slightly (response score of 20). Both perceived the White person as a *social worker* (response scores of 48 and 52). On the other hand, the Blacks were more likely to perceive *concern* or *understanding* (response score of 61) than were the Whites (response score of 15). They were also more likely to perceive *conflict* (response score of 43 for the Blacks as opposed to 6 for the Whites). The *need* or *help* component did not vary much (147 for the Blacks, 110 for the Whites). In short, both groups perceived the situation as one of helping, probably in some institutionalized form, such as social work. The Blacks were much more likely than were the Whites to perceive the relation as affective, and they were more ambivalent about it. They perceived the relation as both *good* and *distrustful*, whereas the Whites perceived it only as *friendly*. Incidentally, it should be pointed out that the response *maid* occurred only in the responses for the Blacks.

The second picture showed a young Black woman and a young White man seated on what appears to be an outdoor chaise lounge. The man is smiling at the woman and holding a bottle of Coca-Cola, which he is about to pour into a glass. The Black woman, who is turned towards the man and away from the camera, is laughing.

The responses to this picture were remarkably similar. The Black group placed more emphasis than did the White group upon the racial identity of the participants in this picture, as, indeed, they did generally. This was one of the pictures with the participants first shown together and then shown separately. To all three presentations, the Blacks achieved a response score of 232 on *Black–White*, whereas the Whites achieved a score of 109. The Blacks were also more likely to identify the participants as *male* and *female* than were the Whites.

The major component for the picture, in all three presentations, was *fun* or *enjoyment* (response score for Blacks = 748, for Whites = 811). The differences in patterns between Blacks and Whites was mainly in the mode of expression rather than the affective content. The White group was more likely to produce *laughter,* and *smiles,* whereas the Black group produced *enjoyment* and *joy*. This is reminiscent of the Black respondents greater tendency to use abstract expressions of *love* in response to the TAT pictures, whereas the Whites more often produced responses indicating concrete actions of *love*. It may well be that there is a greater Black emphasis upon inner feeling. If we look at the total response scores for all 30 pictures, we see that the Blacks produced higher response scores for *love, understanding, happy, joy, good time, content,* and *ease,* whereas the White respondents produced higher scores for *enjoy, fun, joke, laughter,* and *smile.*

The associative affinity scores for all 30 pictures were subjected to a factor analysis, using the revised BMDX72 program developed by the Health Sciences Computing Facilities at UCLA. With a constant value of .30, the analysis produced six factors that were submitted to a varimax rotation. Presenting the factor

TABLE 5.4

Summed Response Scores for Pictures Showing Black–White Interactions

Domain: man and woman

Black scores:	1296	(man, 494; woman, female, etc., 581; brother, 141)
White scores:	870	(man, 306; woman, female, etc., 413; girl, 151)

Domain: racial identity

Black scores:	1352	(Black, 588; White, 557; integration, 56; African, 152)
White scores:	817	(Black, 482; White, 236; integration, 17; African, 17)

Domain: interpersonal relations

Black scores:	1174	(love, 453; understanding, 113; togetherness, 164; hate, 39; friend, 345; concern, 33; touch, 27)
White scores:	1118	(love, 276; understanding, 33; togetherness, 45; friend, 505; concern, 66; closeness, 100; touch, 61; gratitude, 32)

Domain: people

Black scores:	628	(people, 68; hippy, 48; doctor, 61; nurse, 371; policeman, 27; businessman, 53)
White scores:	557	(people, 8; doctor, 11; nurse, 316; policeman, 88; businessman, 134)

Domain: human characteristics

Black scores:	128	(beautiful, 41; attractive, 9; young, 50; hands, legs, 28)
White scores:	703	(attractive, 133; quiet, 64; young, 173; blond, 132; hands, legs, 168; mustache, 32)

Domain: recreation

Black scores:	316	(picnic, 98; pool, 105; swim, 10; camp, 7; play, 66; summer, 30)
White scores:	490	(picnic, 36; pool, 183; swim, 60; camp, 47; play, 95; summer, 69)

Domain: feelings, moods

Black scores:	2030	(happy, 725; joy, 190; good time, 73; content, 57; ease, 45; enjoy, 121; fun, 254; joke, 52; laughter, 207; smile, 259; tease, 28; surprised, 19)
White scores:	2229	(happy, 564; joy, 39; good time, 30; content, 27; ease, 45; enjoy, 170; fun, 344; joke, 136; laughter, 385; smile, 343; tease, 65; surprised, 49; bored, 32)

(continued)

TABLE 5.4 *(continued)*

Domain: needs, problems
  Black scores: 333   (need, 125; money, 94; sick, 114)
  White scores: 39   (money, 7; sick, 32)

Domain: sex
  Black scores: 185   (sex, 164; seductive, 21)
  White scores: 243   (sex, 94; seductive, 74; flirt, 75)

Domain: education
  Black scores: 202   (teach, 133; discussion, 29; lecture, 40)
  White scores: 313   (teach, 99; discussion, 85; lecture, 90; college, 39)

Domain: hospital
  Black scores: 219   (hospital, 219)
  White scores: 178   (hospital, 178)

loadings would be meaningless without the pictures themselves, but a brief summary is in order.

Factor I for the Blacks showed high loadings on Black—White pictures containing a man and a woman. All of these involved some degree of intimacy, with sexual overtones. No such pattern emerged in the factor structure for the White respondents. Factor II for the Blacks was highly loaded on a series of three pictures involving hospital scenes. This was equivalent to the first factor for the Whites. Factor II for the Whites was a male sex role factor, as was Factor IV for the Blacks. Factor III for the Whites and Factor III for the Blacks was a factor concentrating on easy, enjoyable relations. It should be noted that the only sizable factor (accounting for more than 10% of the variance) in both instances was Factor I. Although this strong Factor I for the Blacks was an intimacy factor, no such factor emerged in the responses of the Whites. Finally, the six factors in the Black matrix accounted for 57% of the variance, and the six factors from the White matrix accounted for 49% of the variance.

Perhaps more revealing than the factor analysis was a tabulation of the total response scores elicited by these pictures, presented in Table 5.4. First, notice that the Blacks were much more likely than were the White respondents to identify the people in the pictures by *sex* or *race*. The abstractness of the Black perception of *interpersonal relationships* contrasts strongly with the White perception in terms of *closeness* and *touch*. *Motives, problems,* and *needs,* including *sex,* was higher for Blacks, although *seductive* and *flirt* were White-only responses. The Whites gave more human characteristics, both psychological and physical, than did the Blacks, the exception being the Black-only response, beautiful.

Shifts in Associative Meaning to Pictures

Finally, we briefly examine some data that comprise a part of an experimental study of shifts in associative meaning to pictorial representations as the result of providing an appropriate context for the pictures. The context in this instance was to present a brief episode from a motion picture; the test picture was a still from the motion picture. Once again, this study involved a comparison between Black and White students and between words and pictures. In this case the 50 Black students were from the District of Columbia Teachers College and the 50 White students from the University of Virginia.

It is instructive in this case to look at response scores for the chief domains before and after exposure to the episode from which the picture was taken. As an example, Table 5.5 shows the scores for the first and second exposure to a picture depicting three people, one White man, one Black man, and one White woman. The two men are looking at each other, and the woman is looking at the Black man on her right. They are all about the same age (early 30s). The film itself is a 30-second episode in which a White couple, Paul and Phyllis, welcome the Black man, George, upon his arrival to attend the university in the

TABLE 5.5

Components of Response Scores Before and After Film Episode
for Picture of Three People Described in Text

| | Black Respondents | | White Respondents | |
Main Components	Before	After	Before	After
Male−Female	100	67	41	21
People	178	54	135	102
Family, home	15	21	39	15
Friendship	132	209	160	222
Meeting, talking	168	193	193	219
Black−White	44	86	3	44
Enjoyment, entertainment	136	44	208	145
Suspicion, prejudice	6	56	−	56
College, education	−	85	16	119
Total components	779	815	795	943
Total response scores	808	857	875	1043

town. When Paul invites George to spend the next day with them, Phyllis reminds Paul that they have another obligation.

Even though reactions to pictures tended to be more concrete than reactions to words, it is clear that the context of the episode gave even greater concreteness to the associations. The domains having to do with abstract and general concepts (*male−female, people*) dominated the first testing. The misconception that the picture was at a party or some similar gathering resulted in a high component of *entertainment* on the initial testing that disappeared almost completely for the Black students, but not for the White students. However, both Black and White students increased the category of responses having to do with *friendship*. It is perhaps surprising that the dominance scores rose only slightly for both groups, more for the White students than for the Black.

The changes reveal one general effect, the greater specificity of responses produced by context, and one subtle effect, the almost complete disappearance of the *entertainment* category for the Black students. The ambivalence created by Phyllis's remark almost completely eliminated the *party* and *socializing* for the Black students. Both the Black and White students produced responses on the after-test of *phony, false, caution, apprehensive, prejudice,* and *anxiety,* responses assigned to the *suspicion−prejudice* category that were completely absent in the initial testing. It is obvious that the point of the episode was not lost on the White students, but they appeared to be reacting to it less affectively than did the Black students.

This investigation examined such before and after distributions for eight pictorial stimuli, eight verbal stimuli, and two episodes. Essentially, the same pattern held for all of the pictorial stimuli. There was an increase in the specificity of responses and, in some instances, a sharp change in the affective reaction. Because both episodes involved Black−White relations, it is not surprising that the changes in affectivity were greater for the Blacks than for the Whites. In all of our investigations, there is evidence of greater affect for stimuli involving race relations for the Black than for the White students. Also, it is not surprising that there was a larger increase in negative affect than in positive affect for the Blacks, given the nature of the episodes. The eight verbal stimuli showed much the same pattern, though in less intensity. There was less affect after the episode, and the words were slightly more resistant to change than the pictures (correlations across the film episodes averaged .60 for pictures and .66 for words).

For the pictures, the similarity between the Black and White groups was almost identical, on the average, before and after the film episodes ($r = .58$ vs. $r = .59$). However, the striking feature of the data is the fact that for both Black and White students, the affinity scores increased after the film episode. The mean affinity scores increased from 12.5 on the first testing to 17.9 on the second (significantly different beyond .01). The increase is about the same irrespective of whether the data came from Black or White respondents or whether the affinity was between words and words, pictures and pictures, or words and pictures.

There was a difference between words and pictures, however, on the relation between the before and after affinity scores. Before and after affinity scores for words were more highly correlated (Black $r = .887$; White $r = .889$) than were the before and after affinity scores for pictures (Black $r = .433$; White $r = .375$). The pattern of the affinity scores was altered more for pictures than for words. The correlations of affinity scores for words and pictures were intermediate and did not depend upon whether it was the pictures first and words second or words first and pictures second (average $r = .480$). Thus, the associations to the pictures and words are influenced about equally by the film, but the words produced a more coherent pattern after the film than did the pictures. Once again, this is almost certainly the result of the fact that the words were responded to as entities, whereas the pictures may have been responded to by parts.

In summary, we must conclude that, for most purposes, words are more useful than pictures in eliciting structures of subjective meaning in the most general possible way. Pictures yield, of course, subjective meaning, and there must be special cases where nothing but a picture or some sort of visual representation will do for a particular purpose. If, however, it is the purpose of the investigation to reveal cultural stereotypes, beliefs, and knowledge, words seem to come closer to eliciting the information people carry in their conceptual structures than do pictorial representations. We have not, in these investigations, examined abstract cultural symbols, such as the swastika, but we would expect these to be more like words than pictures. They have the conceptual unity of words. Pictures, on the other hand, are like linguistic sequences. They are specific, are readily decomposable into their elements and, as the comparison earlier in this chapter showed, behave associatively more like phrases than like concepts represented by words in isolation.

6

Inferences About Attitudes

Part of the psychological meaning of things in our subjective world is the posture or attitude we take towards them. Because these attitudes are so important to our social life, psychologists have long segregated them out for special attention. The investigation and measurement of attitudes is one of the most venerable enterprises in social psychology. Because of the special interest in attitudes, we use this chapter to demonstrate ways of extracting information about them from associative data. We also try to draw the implications of the principle that the affective associative meaning of a stimulus is reflected by the aggregate affective meaning of the responses. Such a notion implies that affectivity may be assumed, irrespective of the specific content from which it comes. But the actual associative responses enable us to examine the semantic content of evaluation, something that is difficult to do with traditional attitude measurement.

ASSOCIATIONS AND AFFECTIVITY

A Linear Model

This notion of the summation of affectivity given by responses in free association is paralleled to some extent by the linear models of attitude expression recently developed by Fishbein (1967) and Ramsey and Case (1970). In these models, the evaluative reaction to a stimulus is a consequence of summing the product of the evaluative reaction to a relevant property and the stimulus scale value on that property across all relevant attitudes. This notion, and its resulting technique of measuring attitudes, has in common with the present conception the view that evaluation or affectivity may be separated from relevant content and that each such separated element may be summed to obtain a measure of the intensity and direction of the evaluative reaction to a stimulus. It is not clear whether either Fishbein or Ramsey and Cross intended their model to be a process model, but we believe process models in this area to be premature. In the present instance we argue that the process of forming and expressing attitudes can only be roughly approximated by our method of obtaining an index of affectivity or evaluation. We do believe that an attitude towards some particular object is the result of our evaluative reactions to all the components or features of that object, but we cannot suppose that this result is precisely paralleled by the summation of affectively coded associative scores or, for that matter, the affective ratings on properties of some stimulus, as in the techniques advocated by Fishbein and by Ramsey and Case. Also, as we have pointed out in connection with other problems, the meanings of things change. Some of these changes are slow and maintain some particular direction for a long period of time. Thus, we may become increasingly favorably disposed towards the idea of gasoline rationing as an energy crisis deepens. But there are shorter fluctuations in meaning, including attitudes, that are conditioned by some particular context. A White person with generally unfavorable attitudes towards Black Americans may temporarily swing in a more positive direction as the result of watching Martin Luther King Sr.'s moving closing prayer at the 1976 Democratic Convention. We believe that associative reactions capture the varieties of different affective reactions towards some particular stimulus as well as their fluctuations more naturally and less self-consciously than do rating scales or any other device that might encourage respondents to be defensive. It is our purpose in this chapter to present evidence in support of this belief.

In Chapter 2 we proposed an index of affectivity that sums all response scores coded affectively positive, subtracts the sum of all response scores coded negatively, and divides by the total response score for the stimulus in question. This index, the evaluative-dominance index, is sensitive to both the proportion of responses that are affective and to their direction. The only weighting is provided by the response score weighting described in Chapter 2. It is possible, of course, to compute an affectivity score for individuals as well as for groups, and we shall have occasion to refer to such a use, but our main interest will center upon summing the response scores across some relatively homogeneous sample of individuals.

Associations and Other Techniques

Before presenting some sample data on associations in the measurement of attitudes, perhaps a word about the naturalness of associations may help explain that, although we should expect associative measures to correlate with more traditional measures, we do not necessarily expect the correlations to be high under all circumstances. Traditional measures require persons to respond to questions such as the following: "Do you agree or disagree with the statement, Medicare will do more harm than good?" The particular response persons give will not only be the result of their best estimate about how they feel about Medicare at the moment but also, to some extent, their estimate of how the world at large will evaluate their response. This has been a problem in attitude measurement from the beginning, and various methods have been proposed to get around it. One of the best known is the "bogus pipeline" (Jones & Sigall, 1971). In this technique subjects are duped into believing that their psycho-physiological responses are being recorded, and these will betray them if they lie. Jones and Sigall showed that responses are changed in a direction such as to suggest that subjects are paying less attention to how people will evaluate their responses when tested under the belief that their true feelings will be detected physiologically. On the other hand, Ostrom (1973) pointed out that the responses obtained by this deception are highly correlated with ordinary rating measures and, indeed, do not differ in pattern very much when subjected to various experimental conditions. The moral being that attempts, by decep-tion, to remove self-evaluation of responses may succeed, but may or may not change the pattern of responses depending upon how one views the results.

With this in mind, we introduce associations as a natural method of obtain-ing attitudes not so much with the notion that the pattern of results may or may not be different from those obtained with rating methods, but with the belief that they provide a richer source of data, particularly when the method of continued association is used. The respondent produces associations express-ing affect but also the semantic features associated with or responsible for that affect.

Finally, although our society is used to the culture of the social sciences, other societies are not. It is by no means obvious that rating scales have univer-sal cultural validity. The tendency of Americans to accept rankings and quantita-tive rating of almost everything under the sun strikes some foreigners as being incomprehensible and even repugnant. The process of free association, on the other hand, is easily understood and requires nothing more culturally unique than the use of a particular language. Furthermore, in many situations, candid-ness may be risky and unpleasant. Such is far more likely to be the case in a politically repressive society than in a free society. Associations, like certain of the jokes that circulate in repressed countries, are sufficiently ambiguous to get by. Associations are not as explicit as making an assertion would be.

Some Association Data

With this much background, we may turn to some smaple data comparing asso-ciative methods of determining attitudes with other methods. For a beginning we turn to an investigation by Szalay, Windle, and Lysne (1970). These investigators compared results achieved as the result of the application of the associative method with results achieved with a form of the semantic differential and with traditional attitude ratings. Szalay et al. presented the correlations between the evaluative-dominance index for individual subjects and the semantic differential, as well as the correlations of the associative measure with attitude ratings for three concepts, *civil rights, Vietnam policy,* and *birth control.* The correlations were positive but low. Only one (*Vietnam policy*) achieved statistical significance for the association measure, compared with both the semantic differential and the rating scale. It is easy to suppose that this outcome is the result of the inherent unreliability of individual evaluative-dominance scores. These scores are subject to all of the variability inherent in any method that depends upon free responding. A single response in the first position can drastically change the resulting evaluative dominance score for a single individual from positive to negative.

This supposition is confirmed by the fact that correlations calculated across 15 concepts, using as data points responses summed across 50 individuals, were high and positive. The correlation between the evaluative-dominance index and the semantic differential was .91; the correlation between the evaluative-dominance index and attitude ratings was .90. In short, data obtained by pooling results from a homogeneous group of persons were stable enough to produce in the evaluative dominance index the same pattern of results as those achieved with the more traditional measures. We must point out, however, that the associative data are perhaps slightly different, for the correlation between the semantic differential rating and the direct attitudinal rating was .97 when calculated across the 15 concepts. Without at this point stopping to present supporting arguments, we suggest that the higher correlation between the two ratings is the result of some more general rating effect (such as the halo effect).

Thus, we have evidence to support the principle that the affective evaluation of a concept can be assessed by summing the positively and negatively coded associations. However, such an assessment is probably less reliable for individuals than are direct methods achieved by ratings, so long as we can suppose that the ratings are uncontaminated by self-conscious evaluations of the ratings themselves. We should remember, as has been pointed out, that this is sometimes a dubious assumption.

Some indirect evidence for the proposition that associative data are less contaminated by self-consciousness about the responses is found in a further study examining the evaluative-dominance index. Here the comparison was with a traditional attitudinal-rating scale and a similar scale obtained under the conditions of a "bogus pipeline." The subjects were first tested in a group, at which time associative data and rating-scale data were obtained on 18 different themes. Several weeks after the group testing, some of the same subjects were tested individually under conditions of a "bogus pipeline." This time the subjects were asked to state their attitudinal positions after being told that "EMG" responses

TABLE 6.1

Number of Subjects Achieving Positive (+), Negative (−), or Neutral (0) Scores on a
Semantic Differential, Attitude Questionnaire, and the Evaluative-Dominance Index

	Semantic Differential			Attitude Questionnaire			Evaluative-Dominance Index		
Concept	+	0	−	+	0	−	+	0	−
Capitalism	46	2	2	46	2	2	33	5	12
Saigon government	18	12	20	21	9	20	10	5	35
Vietnam policy	28	3	19	28	3	19	16	8	26
Birth control	47	2	1	49	0	1	32	15	3
Civil rights	43	3	4	44	2	4	33	6	11
Abortion	30	6	14	32	1	17	12	3	35
Federal school Aid	45	0	5	43	1	6	31	8	11
Foreign aid	38	3	9	40	1	9	26	7	17
Medicare	34	4	12	32	3	15	25	14	11
Socialism	24	7	19	20	4	26	14	15	21

were being recorded and that these would reveal their real choices. Six of the themes (*Blacks, Malcolm X, Woman's lib, Female equality, Marijuana,* and *Getting high*) were the same as in the original testing.

Not surprisingly, the correlation between the evaluative-dominance indices for individual subjects and their attitude ratings was higher than that between the evaluative-dominance indices and the ratings obtained under the conditions of the "bogus pipeline" ($r = .66, p < .01$, vs. $r = .21$). However, what is interesting is the pattern of comparisons of ratings on the attitude questionaire with the responses under the "bogus pipeline" and the evaluative-dominance indices. In conformity with the data reviewed by Jones and Sigall (1971), the ratings under the "bogus pipeline" condition were less positive than those under the standard conditions of attitude measurement. For 24 subjects on the six themes, a total of 70 measures were the same, 44 were less positive, and 29 were less negative. A comparable pattern of results happened when the evaluative-dominance index was the object of comparison with the "bogus pipeline" procedure. Compared with the standard attitude measure, 30 responses were the same (either positive or negative) on the associative measure, 61 were less positive, and 35 were less negative. The greater variability in the attitude measure-association comparison is to be expected, since the correlation between these measures was less than the correlation (.82) between the attitude measure and the "bogus pipeline" measure. The point is that the associative measure behaves like the "bogus pipeline."

There is a general tendency for the evaluation-dominance index to be more negative than direct attitude measurements. Table 6.1, modified from Szalay et al. (1970), compares the number of subjects (out of 50) achieving positive, negative, and neutral scores on attitudes towards 10 different concepts. It is clear that, with the exception of *medicare* and *socialism*, all of the concepts were evaluated negatively more often by the evaluative-dominance index than by the semantic differential or direct questionnaire methods. All differences between the evaluative-dominance index and the two direct measures were significant except those for *medicare* and *socialism*. In the case of the issues on which there might be some public pressure to be positive (e.g., *civil rights, federal school aid*), there were large differences. There was also a large difference for the concept *abortion*. Here, we may speculate that an attitude splits. Many subjects may agree that abortions are necessary and thus rate the concept as positive on the semantic differential, but the actual process is repellent, and, therefore, the associations to the concept are largely negative, even though such mildly positive response as *necessary* may occur.

The Evaluative-Dominance Index as an Attitude Measure

In summary, an evaluative-dominance index as a measure of the affectivity of responses to some stimulus behaves in the same general way as direct rating scales. Such an index is probably too unreliable to use for individual subjects (any investigation using regression on individual subjects as the major tool would better either avoid altogether the evaluative-dominance index or modify the method of continued association to obtain more data on individual subjects; see Chapter 8), but it shows a high correlation with ratings when group measures are correlated across themes or concepts. Furthermore, when subjects change their ratings as the result of the "bogus pipeline" condition, they are apt to show similar deviations in evaluative measures derived from associations. Finally, there is a tendency for the evaluative-dominance index to be negative more often than is the case for direct measures.

These results are encouraging so far as the use of associative data in the measurement of attitudes is concerned. Of course, as we discuss later in this chapter, the major information provided by associations in the study of attitudes is in the content of the responses rather than their position on some scale of affectivity. However, it would be desirable if it were possible to improve the measure of evaluation for individuals derived from the method of continued association. To that end, several variations on scoring the responses have been tried, all without conspicuously different results. However, more drastic modification of the method of collecting data may prove to be more promising (Chapter 8).

There are several problems with individual evaluative-dominance indices. First, out of the typical seven or eight responses emitted by a given subject, only one or two of them may be evaluative in nature. Second, the responses must be coded by someone. The coding process itself may be unreliable, and in any case, in the data reported thus far, the responses have been simply coded positive or negative. Greater discriminability might well be achieved if the coders were allowed to weight the response in some way. Finally, it is possible that the subjects themselves may be better judges of the affectivity of their own responses than are independent coders. All of these considerations enter into the comparisons. To make a long story short, weighting the responses by intensity slightly increases the correlations of the evaluative-dominance index, with standard attitude ratings and with connotative ratings of the semantic differential sort, as does combining themes into domains, but the improvement is marginal. No correlations differ by more than .15. However, allowing subjects to judge their own affectivity scores reduces the correlations, in some instances fairly drastically. Clearly, allowing subjects to second guess their responses is a mistake.

ASSOCIATIONS AND INTERPRETATION OF ATTITUDES

Why make use of the more time-consuming associative method if all it does is provide a somewhat greater tendency to produce (unpopular) negative evaluations? The answer is that, in fact, the associative method does produce more than this; it produces richer data. In some respects, data obtained by the method of continued association achieves the depth and variety attained by unstructured interviews, without the problems attendant upon reducing the data from unstructured interviews to some unbiased summary. In the context of determining evaluation in attitudes, it is possible to determine which features are responsible for the positive and negative attitudes held by the persons responding through application of the associative method. One of the weaknesses of the linear models presented by Fishbein (1967) and Ramsey and Case (1970) is that they require investigators to invent the features or dimensions that they think might be significant sources of affective evaluation for the respondents. Using the associative method, it is possible to let the respondents themselves tell us what the significant sources of affect are. It is possible, therefore, if traditional methods are preferred, that associative data may provide empirical basis for the choice of features to be rated.

An Example

These possibilities can be illustrated by an analysis of the responses to the concept *socialism*. Two groups of students were formed on the basis of their evaluative ratings of the concept *socialism*. One group of 49 students all exhibited varying degrees of positive response to the concept, whereas another group of 49 exhibited either neutral or negative evaluations by ratings. Of the subjects indicating positive evaluation, 4 were highly positive, 19 were moderate, and 26 slightly positive. For the other group, 13 were highly negative, 13 were moderate, 12 were slightly negative, and 11 were neutral. The evaluative-dominance

TABLE 6.2

Main Components of the Reactions to Socialism for Groups Showing
Positive and Negative Ratings towards the Concept

| | Category Scores | |
Response Category	Positive Subjects	Negative Subjects
Marx, communist leaders, theoreticians	35	83
Other persons, people	61	48
United States	29	0
Communist countries	41	92
Noncommunist countries	120	89
Freedom, equality	53	35
Positive evaluative terms	123	44
Negative evaluative terms	53	179
Marxism, communism, communist	98	167
Other "isms," political doctrines	82	45
Government, politics, power	161	122
Economics	137	151
Social welfare	53	55
Social groupings, professions	68	21
Miscellaneous	75	86
Total response scores	1189	1217

indices for the two groups, determined by a coding of the associative responses by two independent judges, were +6.6 for the group giving positive ratings and −10.4 for the group giving negative evaluations. The important matter, however, is not the evaluative responses, but the distribution of the other responses between the two groups. These data are presented in Table 6.2.

Table 6.2 reveals that positive and negative respondents understand socialism differently. As a group, the negative raters tended to think of *socialism* more in connection with *Marx, Marxism,* and *communism* than did the positive raters. The positive responders showed higher response scores on *non-Communist countries* (*Sweden, England,* etc.), *United States,* and *Political doctrines other than Communism* and on *persons* and *people other than communists.* In short, the positive raters made a differentiation between socialism and communism that was only weakly made by the negative raters.

The Extent of Evaluation

One important characteristic of the use of associative measures in making inferences about attitudes is that it is possible to determine from them the extent to which a given concept evokes attitudes. We may be fairly said to have attitudes towards most things (that is the reason why the evaluative factor on the semantic differential nearly always turns out to have the highest loading of

TABLE 6.3

Proportion of Response Scores and the Evaluative-Dominance
Indices Given over to Evaluation for Six Different Concepts

Concept	Proportion Evaluation Responses	Evaluative-Dominance Index
Freedom	14.5	+14.5
Law	6.5	+ 4.3
United States	23.8	+22.1
Marijuana	16.4	−12.0
Mental illness	13.7	−12.8
Psychiatrist	7.9	+ 5.3

any factor on most all stimuli), but we surely feel more strongly about some things than others. The best way to determine the intensity of the feelings about some concept held by some group of persons is to total all of the evaluative responses, irrespective of sign, and determine the proportion these are of the total response score. Table 6.3 compares the evaluative-dominance index for six concepts with a measure of the percentage of the total response score given over to evaluative responses. These data were obtained from 156 White residents of Washington, D.C.

The total evaluative response scores ranged from a high of 23.8% for *United States* to 6.5% for *law*. In general, these respondents appear to be fairly conservative. Their evaluative-dominance index was highly positive for *United States* and almost equal to the total evaluative-response score (the era was that of the Vietnam war, when there was a lot of criticism of the United States). The evaluative-dominance index for *marijuana* was negative, and only a small portion of the total evaluative response score to that stimulus was negative.

For these six concepts, there was a high correlation between the magnitude of the total evaluation scores and the total evaluative-dominance index, though, of course, the sign of the evaluative-dominance index varies. However, that is not necessarily the case. Interesting in this respect is a comparison of the total evaluation scores and the evaluative-dominance indices for the reactions to two individuals, *Martin Luther King, Jr.* and President *Carter*. The data on *Martin Luther King, Jr.* were obtained from 50 students at the University of Maryland; the data on President *Carter*, from 50 University of Virginia undergraduates. The total evaluative score for *Martin Luther King, Jr.* was 26.2, and all the evaluative responses were positive, with the result that the evaluative-dominance score was identical to the total of evaluative responses. The total evaluative score for President *Carter* for the Virginia students was 17.7%, but the evaluative-dominance index was almost precisely 0 (0.01). In short, although an attitudinal stance is an important component in both the reaction to *Martin Luther King, Jr.* and to President *Carter*, the attitude in one case was totally positive, whereas in the other case it was almost perfectly ambivalent.

The Semantic Content of Attitudes

It needs to be said, however, that no single measure or single set of measures exhausts the potential of associative data for telling us something about the stance of a particular group of people towards a given theme. The comparison of *Martin Luther King, Jr.* and President *Carter* is again relevant. The responses to *Martin Luther King, Jr.* give evidence of clearly focused understanding of him and his role in American history. Almost all the responses centered on his personal attributes and the role he played in the civil rights struggle. Responses indicating his relation to other people (*Robert Kennedy, Coretta King, James E. Ray*) totaled to a response score of only 48. In contrast, President Carter's image was heavily influenced by the publicity received by his family. Relevant people (we must segregate relevance here because certain responses indicated that the respondents were thinking of some friend or acquaintance named *Carter* some of the time) achieved a response score of 205, of which 163 were given over to members of the President's family and 42 to political associates. To the extent that there was a sharp image of his accomplishments in the minds of these Virginia students in the summer of 1977, it centered more on *foreign* affairs (response score of 20) and *winning* the election (22) than anything else. However, the total of what might be called a domain of *political action* was only 83 for President *Carter*. In contrast, the total action domain for *Martin Luther King, Jr.* was 262, of which 208 centered on achieving *civil rights* and *marching*. Furthermore, the political image projected by President *Carter* was diffuse. He was perceived as being *liberal, moderate,* and *conservative*, as well as being a *populist*.

Since we began this chapter with a reference to the current interest among students of attitude measurement in multicomponent additive models of evaluation in attitudes, it will be instructive to compare the nature of the evaluative responses for *Martin Luther King, Jr.* and for President *Carter. Strong, intelligent, determined, peaceful, hero, good, great, humanitarian* provide a fair sampling of the positive responses to *Martin Luther King, Jr.* There were no negative responses, of course, and the comparatively mild positive terms (*interested, helpful*) accounted for a very small percentage of the total evaluative scores. The positive terms for President *Carter* were more of a mixture. They ranged from *careful* and *interesting* through *guiding, ingratiating,* and *faithful* to *intelligent, determined,* and *decisive*. Unlike the case for *Martin Luther King, Jr.,* for whom many of the evaluative terms individually achieved high scores, the evaluative scores for President *Carter* were individually low and scattered. Once again, his image is diffuse compared with that of King. President Carter's negative terms were clearly of two kinds, outright epithets such as *hick, red-neck, jerk,* and *ass hole,* and such descriptive adjectives as *inept, disappointing, wishy-washy,* and *inexperienced*. It is interesting to note that many of the negative terms were in direct contradiction to the positive ones. Thus, negative reactors saw President *Carter* as being *nondecisive* and *noninformed*.

As a final word on evaluation in connection with these data, it should be noted that some characteristics that ordinarily would not be considered to be necessarily evaluative are, by context, evaluative. Several of the respondents who characterized Mr. Carter as *liberal* did so in a context of many negative descriptors. One must infer that to these respondents, *liberal* is a term of opprobrium. We deal at greater length in Chapter 8 with the question of the correlations among responses from a single respondent.

This comparison between the responses on the part of college students to *Martin Luther King, Jr.* and President *Carter* is not intended to contrast the two men or the two samples but rather to point out how associative data can capture qualitative differences in attitudes. The image of *Martin Luther King, Jr.* might be expected to be relatively clear and sharp. The image projected by a new president, less than a year in office, one who won by a slim majority, is expected to be diffuse and equivocal. One may speculate, however, that President *Carter* may be more favorably regarded by this sample of college students than were any of his last three predecessors.

Further illustration of the ability of the associative method to reveal the semantic components of evaluation is provided by a return to the associative distributions to the six concepts presented in Table 6.3. In each instance, evaluation occurred in conjunction with several characteristic semantic features, although the ubiquitous *good–bad* contrast (and its synonyms) always managed to be present, and in most instances dominated. Such, for example, was the case with the concept, *marijuana*, which, for our White Washington, D.C. respondents, produced a response score of 125 for *bad* and 45 for *good*. However, in addition, it was clear that *marijuana* is *bad* because it leads to *addiction* (response score of 35), may lead to *illness* (response score of 38) and is *harmful* (response score of 52). This was not the only semantic cluster associated with the negative evaluation of *marijuana*. For some of our respondents it is *evil* (response score of 21), a *sin* (25) and just plain *wrong* (20). It also leads to *trouble* (17), is a *problem* (10), and *unnecessary* (11). On the positive side, it is associated with *fun* (23) and being *high* (21).

Mental illness is *bad* (26), but it is also *shameful* (11), a *sin* (14), *sad* (99), and leads to *sorrow* (10). The *law* had less of an evaluative component associated with it, but what there was reveals it as being *necessary* and *helpful*. For a few people it must be *unfair* and *wrong*. *Freedom*, as a concept, was perceived as being necessary and associated with *happiness* and *liberty*. It produced no negative responses from these samples. The *United States* was *great*, *beautiful*, and *free*.

There were, as we have just noted, some surprises in these data, and there were some responses that must cause a sense of disappointment in those who are concerned with the attitudes held by people at large. It is not surprising to learn that *marijuana* has a component of *sin*, but it is disappointing to learn that *mental illness* is still associated with *sin* and *shame*. Although it is perhaps more a matter of the subjective knowledge and beliefs of the respondents than their attitudes, it should be noted, in this connection, that there is a fair-sized component of *born* or *birth* in the reactions of our respondents to *mental illness.*

Thus, while the evaluative-dominance index presents us with information about attitudes comparable to that obtained from the more traditional techniques of attitude measurement, techniques such as those that ask questions of respondents or ask them to evaluate various concepts, it is also the case that a qualitative analysis of associative data presents us with information about the semantic features associated with evaluation, features that may, in fact, be responsible for the evaluation. In many cases, drawing upon either general social psychological theory or upon some empirical evidence, we may infer that these semantic features reflect the subjective reasons, causes, or motivational roots of positive or negative evaluation. Furthermore, they sometimes provide us with a clue as to the reasons for the poor correspondence between verbally expressed attitudes and behavior. Here, the descriptive terms applied by respondents are helpful, whereas the epithets they produce tend only to give an indication of the intensity of their reactions.

Given what we know about the use of marijuana in society today, it was initially surprising to see that marijuana achieved a relatively high net negative evaluative-dominance index. We may speculate that our sample was probably mixed with regard to both use of and attitude towards marijuana. The negativity seems to stem from an awareness on the part of the Washington, D.C. residents of its potential toxicity (whether there is a real medical danger from marijuana is not the issue; it is clear that such a danger was in the back of the minds of these respondents) and also that there was a strong component of *sin* and *weakness.* All these negative features, which outnumber positive reactions about *marijuana*, however, may be put aside by a given individual when its pleasure, real or contemplated, is imagined. Although there are undoubtedly within-individual correlations in affectivity (see Chapter 8), it is inevitably the case that the same individual will exhibit both positive and negative reactions.

Because our actions are multiply determined, in the sense of being dependent upon a variety of attitudes as well as situational conditions, we should not expect that our knowledge and attitudes towards our knowledge would predict behavior in any simple way. We would not expect a moderate to heavy user of alcohol or tobacco to be completely negative towards these substances in verbally expressed attitudes, perhaps, but we should not be surprised if the verbal expressions, including associations, contain more negative and more intense negative than positive responses. In short, it would in no way surprise anyone to find that attitudes, in these cases, would appear to contradict behavior. Attitudes themselves are complex and ambivalent. Furthermore, they may often be at odds with motives, and it should be said that attitudes may well contradict motives. In general, we may well expect internal contradictions in the subjective representational system. As we have pointed out earlier, it is neither particularly logical nor rational.

The chief advantage of the associative method in the study of attitudes is in the richness of the semantic base for evaluative reactions that it provides. It does correlate with the more traditional measures, but in determining evaluation itself, has no particular advantage and may even have the disadvantage of somewhat lower reliability. But the richness of the semantic base provides us with plausible hypotheses about the causes of evaluative reactions to critical concepts and suggests what other concepts such evaluations may be associated with in the minds of the respondents.

A COMPARATIVE STUDY OF POLITICAL ATTITUDES

As alluded to above, beliefs and opinions may be inferred from associative distributions as well as from attitudes. These are part of the total subjective representation of a concept, and in an associative analysis, it is possible to segregate these. We saw earlier that certain associative responses give us reason to suppose that some of the Washington, D.C. residents associated *mental illness* with innate causes. A better arena within which to demonstrate the use of associative distributions to extract information about beliefs and opinions, however, is provided by a comparative study of political concepts. This study compares the responses to certain political concepts by Yugoslavian students at the University of Ljubljana and American students at the University of Maryland. Once again, the comparative approach highlights the differences in dominance rather than outright qualitative differences in the subjective meaning.

Background for an American-Slovenian Comparison

Ljubljana is the capital of the Slovenian republic, with a University of rich historical tradition. Of the six federated republics of Yugoslavia, Slovenia is the most highly developed, with the highest average level of income and education. It is the northernmost republic and, like two other republics, was part of the Austrian Empire until 1918. Its history, ever since the formation of Yugoslavia after World War I, is characterized by recurrent independence movements and, during World War II, by partisan activity. Although students at Ljubljana University cannot be taken as representative of Yugoslavian students generally, given the heterogeneity of the confederation of six republics, they provide an obvious contrast with the students at the University of Maryland. Maryland students are probably more representative of American students, although given the fact that a large proportion of them come from the metropolitan Washington, D.C. area, they are probably politically more sophisticated than students at other, comparable state universities.

Comparative studies of contrasting systems of political orientation offer insights into the nature of belief systems that investigations limited to single social systems do not. Because the American political—economic system is a pragmatic one and communism, even of the comparatively pragmatic Yugoslavian brand, is heavily ideological, we might expect a strong pragmatic—ideological contrast to emerge. Also, we should expect the life situations of the two groups to provide some contrast in their reaction to political ideas. The Harvard studies of Soviet citizens (Bauer, 1959; Inkeles & Bauer, 1961) revealed an emphasis upon order, acceptance of a principle of authority, rejection of certain manifestations of freedom, collectivistic orientation, strong emphasis upon society and social justice, and faith in communistic ideas despite frequent disillusionment with the practical aspects of the Soviet system. Given the geographical proximity and the socialistic ideological orientation, we may expect Slovenian students to be closer to Soviet citizens than to American students at the University of Maryland. The following brief comments are derived from a study narrower in scope than the Harvard study, but it does provide some information about the commitments, beliefs, and opinions of the Americans and their Yugoslavian counterparts.

The American and Slovenian Data Compared

As in most studies reported earlier, each sample consisted of 50 persons, evenly divided by sex. These individuals reacted to a number of concepts, 12 of which had primarily political relevance. They were: *communism, Marxism, socialism,* and *capitalism*, representing the domain of ideology; *president, government, politics,* and *political party*, representing the domain of political institutions; and *peace, freedom, equality*, and *security*, representing political values. Each group received the concepts and responded in their native language.

Communism (*Komunizem*) was strongly positive for the Slovenian students and largely negative for the Americans, as we might expect. *Equality, peace, justice,* and *freedom* were common responses for the Slovenians, but not for the Americans. The total negative response score for the Slovenians was only 4. It is, perhaps, a naive expectation of Americans that individuals living under communistic systems will necessarily be critical of them when given the opportunity. There are dissenters in the Soviet Union, as is well known, and there are probably dissenters in Yugoslavia as well. What the number of dissenters may be is anyone's guess. Furthermore, it is possible for people to be critical of some particular characteristics of the regime without rejecting communism. Those who think of communism as a political ideal frequently criticize the contemporary system by pointing out that it does not meet ideal expectations.

The pragmatic-ideological contrast between the Slovenians and the Americans comes through in the responses to all the ideological stimuli. People associated with *communism* for the Slovenians were *Tito* and *Lenin*, whereas for the Americans, they were *Marx* and *Kruschev* (the data were gathered in 1967).

For both the Americans and the Slovenians, there was a small negative component to *socialism* (*Socializem*). This is surprising, for, as we have just pointed out, there was virtually nothing to suggest negative reactions to *Marxism* or *communism* on the part of the Slovenians. The nature of the responses (*deception, exploitation*) suggests that for some respondents, *socialism* is a sham. To deepen the problem, the Slovenians only mentioned their own country, *Yugoslavia*, and the *Soviet Union* in response to *socialism*, whereas the Americans mentioned *England, Sweden*, and other Western European countries. As with the nature of the *Utopia* and *future* responses of the Slovenians, this is a mystery that cannot be solved with a context-free analysis of associations. In a latter chapter, we point out how taking into account the other responses made to the same stimulus serves sometimes to solve such problems.

Capitalism (*Kapitalizem*) elicited more negative characteristics from the Slovenians than from the Americans, of course. For both the Slovenians and the Americans, however, *capitalism* was associated both with *affluence* and *poverty* (additionally with *famine* for the Slovenians). As with all of the ideological concepts, the Slovenians referred more consistently than did the Americans to *society, classes, workers,* and *proletariat* to the concept *capitalism*. These ideological stimuli made the American students think more frequently of *political organizations*. American responses centered more on *power*, whereas those of the Slovenians centered on *authority*.

The responses to *peace* (*Mir*) were quite similar in the two groups. The differences were the result of the then current American concern with the *war* in *Vietnam* and with the fact that the Slovenians use the same concept (*Mir*) to describe quiet and rest. However, the familiar personal vs. ideological differences emerged in response to the concept *freedom* (*Svobodo*). The Americans gave *liberty, independence,* and *happiness*; the Slovenians produced *peace, equality,* and *brotherhood*. To the concept of *equality* (*Enakost*), the *civil rights* struggle was very much a concern of the Americans. The Slovenians responded with *society* and *state*. Responses to *security* (*Varnost*) once again showed a heavy personal concern on the part of the Americans. Also, the Slovenian concept had a slightly different meaning, which produced responses Americans would more likely associate with *safety*.

If we look at the dominance scores across all stimuli as a measure of the extent to which domains and themes are central to these two groups, we see that the general picture we have produced is confirmed. The Slovenians produced much higher response scores to the ideological stimuli than to either the political institutions or political values, whereas the Americans were more evenly distributed, producing more responses to political values than to the other two. The highest scoring single theme for the Slovenians was *capitalism* whereas the highest scoring theme for the Americans was *peace*, followed by *security*, which produced the lowest response scores for the Slovenians.

In summary, associative distributions can be used to produce many different kinds of information about attitudes, beliefs, and opinions. They can produce a measure of the direction and strength of affectivity, but, more importantly, they provide us with clues as to the basis for the predominant affective stance taken by a group. Furthermore, they tell us what aspects of a concept, whether evaluative in nature or not, are important. Finally, they give us hints about what individuals believe about particular concepts. Here, we should say, it is probably more important to establish a context, and we return to this matter in a later chapter.

7

A Comparison of Associations and Other Methods

In preceding chapters we have presented an account of the varieties of uses to which associative data may be put. We have, in various places, compared associative data with data obtained by other means. We intended such comparisons to be ways of establishing a kind of concurrent validity for the method of continued association. However, in the main, our emphasis has been simply upon presenting the associative data. We have tried to let the reader see, in the context of expected cultural differences, what kinds of information associative data can produce. In this chapter, for the most part, we reverse the emphasis and devote most of the presentation to comparisons of associative data with data obtained by the more or less familiar techniques of psychological investigation.

THE STUDY OF THE SUBJECTIVE LEXICON

First, we consider some comparisons of the associative method with other methods of discovering the semantic structure behind groups of words. Most techniques invented by psychologists for the purpose of discovering the subjective meaning of words have been aimed at creating some kind of subjective lexicon; that is, a dictionary reflecting what is in the head rather than what is out of nature. Of course, any dictionary must somehow reflect human cognitive abilities as well as knowledge about nature. Even so obvious a fact as that most dictionaries are alphabetized by the first letter of words and not by the last tells us something about how human beings process semantic and phonetic (or graphemic) information.

Scaling from Similarity and Associations

Fillenbaum and Rapoport (1971) provided us with the most extensive review to date of the major methods that have been used in the investigation of the semantic relations among words. The only two investigations explicitly comparing associations with other methods of determining semantic relations cited by Fillenbaum and Rapoport are those of Clark (1968) and Henley (1969). Clark examined the use, in the context of sentences and phrases, of prepositions. He showed that a matrix of similarity judgments among English prepositions correlated positively with: (a) the frequency with which a given preposition can substitute for others, (b) classes of objects of prepositions, (c) the results of a grouping task, and (d) free associations. The correlations among the methods were not particularly large, but they were statistically significant. Henley reported on (a) similarity scaling based upon triad judgments, (b) relative rank order in a listing task, (c) pair judgments, and (d) associations of a group of animal names. The correlations among these tasks were higher than in Clark's study, and Henley concluded, despite some differences, that these various procedures for determining the principal features relating the set of words she used all yield essentially the same result. As with Clark, Henley seemed to prefer the results of multidimensional scaling based upon similarity judgments, but little in the way of strong reasons were given for her preference. Both Henley and Clark used discrete association and employed factor analyses of the resulting matrix of overlap coefficients to determine the associative structure of the word lists.

Continued Association and other Methods

No published comparisons exist, however, of matrices of data derived from a continued-association task with other methods of studying the semantic relations among a set of words. The next few pages are given over to such a comparison. At the same time we use the opportunity to, once again, argue that data-reduction techniques taking advantage of correlations within a matrix based upon a set of words often produce their results at the expense of eliminating information of interest.

The study[1] reported here was based upon data provided by 60 University of Maryland undergraduates. These subjects engaged in five tasks, each designed to explore the semantic relations among a set of 12 words. The tasks and words were interspersed among other tasks in order to provide interest and diversity for the subjects. The 12 words were chosen to represent four domains that were,

---

[1]It is perhaps the case that a factor analysis is not the ideal automatic data-reduction technique to accomplish our purpose. But there are difficulties with all such data-reduction techniques applied to semantic relations. This, in part, is an inherent result of the fact that semantic relations involve different kinds of relations.

themselves, fairly widely separated. As has been noted before (Deese, 1975), a clever person can see a semantic relation between any word and almost any other. Nevertheless, the 12 words come from four semantic domains that are not close in meaning. The words were: *food, hunger, rice, money, poverty, beggar, school, knowledge, education, greeting, politeness,* and *manners.* The tasks were: (a) continued association to each word, (b) judgment of similarity among triads of words, (c) a modified word-grouping task, (d) substitution of words in phrases, and (e) judgment of degree of relation. In addition, all subjects rated the words on a standard semantic differential.

The similarity judgment task was like that used by other investigators of semantic relations. The substitution task was a modification of the task used by Stefflre et al. (1971) and others. In the present case, subjects were asked to choose among the 12 words for those that could reasonably substitute for a phrase or sentence built around 1 of the 12 words. The grouping or classification task was modified in order to allow for group administration. For the degree-of-relationship task, subjects were asked to rank order the degree of relation between a given word and the others. This was similar to the listing method used by Henley (1969). The data for all tasks were reduced to a 12 x 12 matrix in which the relationships between each word and all the others were entered. For the associative task, the measure of relation was an overlap score based on associative affinity (Chapter 2).

These matrices were correlated, and the results are shown in Table 7.1. The semantic differential showed an essentially zero correlation with the other measures. This was expected, since the semantic differential forces a semantic analysis with respect to certain pre-fixed features, features that may not be relevant to the internal structure of the set of words under investigation. The other methods were all positively correlated and, despite the small number of words, either approached or exceeded the .05 level of confidence. The correlations were consistent with those achieved by Clark (1968) and by Henley (1969), although they were rather larger. That can be attributed partly to the fact that Clark and Henley each studied a single semantic (or grammatical, in the case of Clark) domain in which the variability of relation from word to word

TABLE 7.1
Correlations among Matrices Obtained from Six
Different Measures of Semantic Relation

Measure	2	3	4	5	6
1. Substitution	.54	.54	.58	.40	−.10
2. Grouping		.82	.91	.84	−.06
3. Similarity judgment			.79	.73	−.24
4. Degree of relation				.77	−.05
5. Associative affinity					−.12
6. Semantic differential					

TABLE 7.2
Factor Loadings on Words by Five Methods for
Measuring Semantic Relations

	Factors			
Method	I	II	III	IV
Association				
Food	.24	−.04	−.78	−.07
Hunger	.32	−.40	−.57	−.29
Rice	.25	.29	−.71	−.17
Money	−.92	−.46	−.05	−.05
Poverty	.27	−.87	.01	−.25
Beggar	.25	−.86	.09	−.23
School	−.91	.15	.22	−.17
Knowledge	−.93	.10	.16	−.13
Education	−.95	.15	.19	−.13
Greeting	.48	.52	.65	−.21
Politeness	.20	.23	.21	.90
Manners	.18	.22	.06	.93
Similarity				
Food	.68	−.30	.59	.14
Hunger	.33	−.78	.40	−.30
Rice	.66	−.29	.64	.19
Money	−.16	−.13	−.92	−.32
Poverty	.16	−.56	−.23	−.74
Beggar	.36	−.13	−.29	−.85
School	−.82	−.44	−.18	.22
Knowledge	−.92	.01	.01	.30
Education	−.94	−.05	−.19	.20
Greeting	.27	.93	.02	.06
Politeness	−.03	.96	.22	.08
Manners	.04	.95	−.20	.04
Substitution				
Food	.97	.10	−.04	.14
Hunger	.35	.31	−.80	−.00
Rice	.92	−.24	.11	.22
Money	.11	.92	−.10	−.19
Poverty	.04	.80	−.38	−.24
Beggar	−.09	.01	−.85	.18
School	−.19	.17	.19	−.93
Knowledge	−.29	.47	.63	.03
Education	−.18	.85	.39	.04
Greeting	−.54	−.25	.20	.48
Politeness	−.70	.02	.60	.23
Manners	−.82	.04	.43	.09
Grouping				
Food	−.78	−.56	−.15	−.08

(continued)

TABLE 7.2 *(continued)*

Method	Factors			
	I	*II*	*III*	*IV*
Hunger	−.71	−.55	.31	.05
Rice	−.64	−.47	−.54	−.22
Money	−.09	−.38	.25	.88
Poverty	−.39	−.34	.71	.43
Beggar	−.26	−.25	.89	.11
School	.92	−.26	−.22	−.04
Knowledge	.91	−.25	−.15	−.21
Education	.96	−.12	−.22	−.15
Greeting	−.12	.91	−.10	−.18
Politeness	−.07	.96	−.14	−.17
Manners	−.04	.96	−.16	−.15
Relationship				
Food	−.72	−.55	−.25	−.30
Hunger	−.74	−.54	−.23	.28
Rice	−.59	−.44	−.43	−.45
Money	.19	−.39	.88	−.02
Poverty	−.53	−.36	.42	.58
Beggar	−.23	−.19	−.07	.91
School	.88	−.27	−.01	−.12
Knowledge	.93	.01	−.06	−.19
Education	.92	−.10	.31	−.18
Greeting	−.09	.82	−.12	−.08
Politeness	.00	.96	−.17	−.10
Manners	.06	.95	−.14	−.12

was about the same and ranged over a large portion of the domain. In the present case, the domains were well separated, and, hence, the regressions were over a larger range of data compared with the within-domain variability.

The matrices for the various methods were subjected to a factor analysis (UCLA Biomed BMDXA-1968 using orthogonal rotation for four factors). Four factors were chosen a priori because the words were originally chosen to represent four separate domains. Interest in the factor analysis centers almost entirely upon the extent to which the analyses of the various matrices reproduce a structure that one might expect, given the nature of the words.[2] The results of the factor analyses are presented in Table 7.2. In general, all methods appeared to have located the words appropriately to varying degrees. Perhaps the associative method did so most successfully, although it succeeded in eliminating the *greeting* concept from the *politeness* domain (which appeared to emerge in Factor IV for this measure). The similarity judgments produced a factor struc-

---

[2]The words were chosen to represent domains, of course, but they were not chosen so as to result in absolutely foregone groupings.

ture close to that expected on a priori grounds, whereas the other three tasks appeared to do so to a lesser degree.

In general, then, these results might be said to be in accordance with the kind of results cited by Fillenbaum and Rapoport (1971). They suggested that, although methods differ, they appear to sort out semantic relations in roughly the same way. Before examining Table 7.2 in detail, however, it is worth while to point out that there is some real advantage to the associative method that may be responsible for some of the features of the factor analysis of associative data presented in Table 7.2. The associative method is not constrained by the particular comparisons the experimenter wishes to make. The other methods all present data in which the relations are determined by the context provided by the total stimulus set. Therefore, it is not surprising that the *politeness* factor (Factor IV) for the associative data did not include *greeting*. *Greeting* is something that would be strongly related to *politeness* and *manners*, as it is in the other data matrices, only when it is in the context of the other words. "Yes," we might say if pressed, "A *greeting* is an act of *politeness*." Left to our own devices, however, *greeting* would belong to *friendship*, rather than *politeness*, etc. The associative method more nearly leaves us to our own devices than do other methods. It was in the context of another culture (Korean) that *greeting* bore a strong associative relation to *politeness*. Since cultural differences in the subjective lexicon are, more often than not, differences in salience, contextually determined methods that minimize salience, such as rating scales or triadic judgments, may obscure or minimize cultural differences.

In a general way, all of the methods behaved reasonably well. For example, all of the methods revealed the cross-domain relations among *hunger, poverty,* and *beggar*. There was, however, certain puzzles. From a semantic point of view, we might question the high Factor II loading that the substitution method produced on the combination *money, poverty,* and *education*, and, in general, the bi-polar relations among factors are not interpretable.

Limitations of the Contextual Methods

However, intuitively satisfying the results, we must question the value of automatic data-reduction techniques, such as factor analysis or multidimensional scaling. The particular associative responses to concepts themselves are more revealing than the internal consistencies among responses to a set of words. It is reassuring to know that the associative affinity matrices do not produce results at odds with methods generally accepted as valid for determining the structure of the subjective lexicon; but the real interest in associative data is provided by the specific responses and families of responses produced. It is important to know that the concepts *educated* and *manners* are more closely related for Colombian than for American students. That fact, however, would scarcely have emerged from any of the contextual methods for studying the subjective lexicon unless we suspected it in the first place and consequently placed *educated* and *manners* in the same list. In short, the various contextual methods are useful for confirming what we might already expect, but the associative method has the potential for telling us something that we had not suspected before.

Although the concept of a subjective lexicon is a useful one, it could only be realized by vast index matrices produced through time-consuming contextual methods. It would be a task of unmanageable proportions to develop a subjective lexicon that would be inclusive enough to be generally useful. Indeed, even with use of the most sophisticated of methods (e.g., triadic similarity judgments) the task would be all but impossible. Some subjective content analysis (Laffal, 1973) may well be the only practical way to provide a data-reduction kind of subjective lexicon.

Finally, the various contextual methods are themselves by and large semantically limited. We pointed out in an earlier chapter that it makes little sense to ask people to judge how similar words such as *food* and *rice* are, and it makes no sense whatever to ask people to group words that have little in common. Yet our contextual methods, applied blindly, ask us to do just that. It is probably the case that our experimental subjects, acquiescent as they are, reinterpret the meaning of such notions as similarity and grouping in order to conform to the demands of the task.

There are reasons why, in this book, we have concentrated on the analysis of responses to words themselves rather than upon trying to reduce the number of dimensions in some semantic field. We have given affinity scores a new use. Rather than being used to show how similar two concepts are (e.g., Deese, 1965; Pollio, 1966), we have employed affinity scores to index the number and salience of relations, possibly qualitatively different relations, between the two concepts in question.

Table 7.2 suggests that we can pull out of associative data much the same information we would have obtained by other methods, but there is additional information. Table 7.1 shows that the semantic differential does not correlate with any of the other methods, including the associative method. But, as Chapter 6 revealed, we can extract from associative data information that is correlated with the major scales of the semantic differential. Because an evaluative index obtained from a single minute of responding is not too reliable, the correlations across individuals between the semantic differential and an evaluative-dominance index (or any other relevant dominance index) will not be high, but the correlations based on group data across words are substantial. In the present instance, the correlation between the semantic differential and the evaluative-dominance index across the 12 words was .76.

THE SUBJECTIVE LEXICON AND SUBJECTIVE CULTURE

Granted, then, that there may be no satisfactory way to discover the structure of the subjective lexicon by the application of some rigorous, universal data-reduction technique, is there any justification for referring to a subjective culture? Can we encompass it? The answers are that the notion is a useful one and that applying associative methods, among others, can, to a greater or lesser degree, make portions of it explicit. The solution in determining the nature of the subjective culture through associative techniques depends upon the level of detail that needs to be resolved. Although the method of continued association does not suffer from the same overwhelming problems of data gathering and treatment than do any of the paired-comparison methods and their derivatives, there are, nevertheless, limits. Fortunately, the major features of subjective meaning in a culture may be appreciated by an analysis of relatively few themes. It is even possible that as few as a dozen themes each, scattered in such significant domains as education and family, may serve to characterize the important subjective components of culture shared in common by persons in that culture. The size of the sample of themes serving as stimuli will depend upon the degree of resolution or grain demanded by a particular investigation and the degree of redundancy tolerated in the interests of obtaining additional information.

A Cross-Cultural Composition

There is another vexing problem, however, when comparing two or more cultures that makes any of the context or comparison methods particularly difficult to apply. The problem is that concepts central to one culture may not be central to another. In Chapter 2 we pointed out how a reasonably comprehensive list of concepts for the purpose of comparing two or more cultures may be arrived at by preliminary testing. Presumably, the same method could be applied to any of the scaling or sorting methods. However, there is a problem for both scaling and sorting methods in this respect. It is clear and obvious that any sorting or grouping depends upon the set of stimuli at hand. The addition of one new concept can lead to an entirely different distribution of categories. It is not yet certain the extent to which the context determined by the set of concepts used in a particular investigation affects the results of multidimensional scaling by similarity. Henley's (1969) data showed invariance of solution when a number of new stimuli were added to her animal name set, but there is no strong theoretical reason for supposing that such a result would always happen. In fact, if a new stimulus introduces or makes particularly prominent some hitherto neglected feature, it should almost certainly cause people to reevaluate their judgments of similarity among the other stimuli. Such concerns, however, do not arise in the largely context-free method of continued association.

   As we pointed out in Chapter 2, there are several ways of arriving at a set of themes suitable for comparing one culture with another. If we wish to examine

TABLE 7.3
Most Frequently Mentioned Important Areas of Life
for American and Korean Students

American Rank Order	Korean Rank	Korean Rank Order	American Rank
1. Love	12	1. Economy	—
2. Friendship	14	2. Religion	—
3. Sex	—	3. Family	4
4. Family	3	4. Job–Occupation	—
5. Education	6	5. Health	19
6. Music	—	6. Education	5
7. Work	12	7. Home	16
8. Marriage	21	8. Friend	—
9. People	—	9. Living	9
10. School	—	10. Offspring–Children	—
11. War	26	11. Interpersonal Rel.	—
12. Money	13	12. Love	1
13. Studying	—	13. Money	12
14. Food	—	14. Friendship	2
15. Travel	15	15. Politics	29
16. Home	7	16. Clothing	16
17. Eating	—	17. Success	—
18. Reading	—	18. Happiness	26
19. Health	5	19. Understanding	—
20. Employment	—	20. Life	—
21. Security	—	21. Marriage	8
22. Freedom	—	22. Hobby	—
23. Sleep	—	23. Language	—
24. Peace	—	24. Character	—
25. Art	—	25. Death	—

cultures at the most general level, we must have some way of determining the central or dominant concerns for that culture. There are, of course, innumerable ways of arriving at such information. One possible way is to do it directly. Table 7.3 lists 25 domains that were most frequently mentioned by a group of Korean students and American students (both in Washington, D.C.). These students were asked to list 25 of the most important problem areas of life. The lists in Table 7.3, which consists of those most frequently mentioned, probably represent an interaction of language and culture. Many of the concepts in one language have no equivalent in another, and so the English versions of the Korean problem areas must be regarded as approximate.

Although these lists reflect the exact wording of the instructions to the subjects, the availability of concepts in the languages, and a host of other specific factors, they could provide a start in a broad cross-cultural investigation of associative meaning for these two cultures. In fact, these stimuli were used as the initial step in preparing a Korean-English lexicon (Szalay, Moon, Lysne, & Bryson, 1971). Preparation of a master stimulus list for such a purpose requires that Korean translations of American concerns not mentioned by the Koreans be added to the list and that English translation of terms unique to the Korean group also be added.

In general, the Korean list, subsequently confirmed by the associative data, revealed a culture that is, in Riesman's (1950) term, more innerdirected than the culture suggested by the American list. When the list in Table 7.3 is expanded by using high-scoring responses as stimuli in turn, characteristic patterns begin to emerge. The Koreans thought more in terms of *people*, for example, in connection with such abstract concepts as *education* than did the Americans. Then too, the notion of *manners* suffused Korean reactions to concepts such as *family, friends,* and even *educated*. Responses that hardly occurred for the Americans, such as *to bow* and *greeting* revealed the stuff that binds Korean personal relations together.

The principal associative responses to *love*, the most frequently listed domain for the Americans, were *sex, peace, marriage, happiness, life, family, girl,* and *mutual*. The Korean equivalent elicited *mother and offspring, offspring, marriage, happiness, woman, friend, brother,* and *parent and offspring*. The greater Korean emphasis upon the *family* is obvious. The principal domains in response to *educated* for the Americans were *cultured, well-rounded, experience,* and *intelligence*, whereas the principal domains for the Koreans were *morality, politeness,* and *dignity*. Incidentally, a later sample (1977 as opposed to 1967) of University of Virginia undergraduates revealed a greater concentration on *intelligence* and *experience* as opposed to being *cultured* and *well rounded* for the Americans, although these all still remained among the principal domains.

In short, by the process of using appropriate data from respondents as a starting point, it is possible to arrive at very general cultural comparisons. These, of course, depend upon translations and the local context of testing. In this connection, we should point out that the Koreans were tested in Washington, D.C. and were undoubtedly more like Americans than would be a group of Koreans of comparable social and educational background who had not been exposed to American culture in an American setting. However, the results conformed to the findings of a later sample of Koreans in Korea, described in Chapter 3.

We began this chapter by pointing out that for those semantic areas that have been examined, associative data and data obtained by the more commonly employed contextual methods yield comparable results. Although this is reassuring, we do not wish to put too much emphasis upon concurrent validity with the scaling techniques as the point of reference. Rather, we would prefer to allow the associative data to stand on their own as being able to represent subjective culture. However, it is customary in psychological (although not necessarily in anthropological) studies to attempt to establish the validity of some new method by reference to established methods or by its ability to confirm testable predictions. Therefore, we have examined the validity of associative data by determining their ability to provide cogent communications within the framework of a culture as well as through a comparison with standard testing techniques. A cogent statement is one that listeners find relevant to their experience. One measure of the cultural appropriateness of associative data is their ability to provide the basis for statements that are regarded by persons from that culture as cogent. An example is provided by the judgments made by another sample of Korean students in Washington, D.C. about pairs of words based upon Korean and American associative norms.

Associations and Communication

A group of 50 Korean students were given pairs of words with each of the stimuli and asked to judge which word goes better with the stimulus. The pairs were derived from high-scoring Korean or high-scoring American responses. For example, for *educated* the choice might be between *smart* (American) and *respect* (Korean). In addition, these same Korean students were given a series of statements based upon the stimulus—response relations in association. There were 144 sentence pairs, half in the form of general statements (e.g., He is smart and educated; he is respectable and educated) and half in the form of appositive statements (e.g., As an educated man he is smart; as an educated man he is respected). For all three types of items, the Koreans chose Korean responses with greater frequency (Szalay, Lysne, & Bryson, 1972). It should be noted that this result occurred despite a specificity in the choice of terms. The response to *poor* was more commonly *ragged*, for example, than *without money*. Yet, if all the responses close to or synonymous with *without money* (*lack, broke, penniless,* etc.) are totaled, they provide a much more important part of the response distribution to *poor* than *ragged* and its synonyms. Furthermore, this study compared only associative norms with associative norms. In a sense it confirms what we are certain of already, namely, that there are cultural differences in association that will be reflected in other activities.

A stronger comparison is that between associative norms and statements devised by people who know the language and culture as area experts. In this case, the comparison was between statements generated from the themes (associative stimuli) by two Americans expert in Korean area studies, each with over 6 years of field experience in Korea, and responses taken from the associative norms. In this case, however, before attempting to construct cogent statements from the associative responses to a particular theme, the related responses were first grouped together. This was done with 13 domains responded to by American and Korean students in Washington. The response lists obtained from the Korean students (in Korean) were translated into English, and all responses obtained from two or more Koreans were grouped together by two Korean graduate students into categories on the basis of similarity of meaning. Next, three sentences were formed to each theme. One was based upon American norms, one

TABLE 7.4
Number of Sentences, Sentence-Sets, and Domains Chosen
as Most Meaningful by Korean Students

| Source | Number of First Choices | | |
	Sentences	Sentence-Sets	Domains
Expert X	607	5	0
Expert Y	679	9	1
Associations[a]	1,376	39	11
Missing choice	38	0	0
Total	2,700	53[b]	12[b]

[a]Only Korean associations were presented to the students for ranking.

[b]One sentence-set and one theme were chosen equally often from associations and from Expert Y.

upon Korean norms, and one obtained from the Korean area experts. The Korean area experts were given statements generated from low-salience associative responses, and they were instructed to generate sentences of the same general type but which would reflect Korean values, experience, and priorities. For example, for the theme *hungry*, the following sentences based upon associations were given to the experts:

Hungry people are frequently farmers (Korean response).
Hungry people are frequently children (American response).
Hungry people are frequently refugees (Korean response).

They were asked to generate two more such sentences. Next, they were asked to rank all sentences for their degree of cogency in the Korean culture. For each of the 13 domains, there were four or five sets of sentences for a total of 54 sets.

A new group of 50 Korean students was given the task of placing the sentences within each set of sentences in rank order. The 54 sets now consisted of three sentences each: One sentence was based upon a high-scoring Korean response category; one sentence was that ranked as most cogent by Expert X; and one sentence was that ranked as most cogent by Expert Y. In choosing the highest-ranking sentence for cogency, the experts were free to pick from Korean or American associative sentences their own productions or the productions of the other expert. The Korean students now ranked the three sentences in each set in terms of how personally meaningful the sentences were to them. The essentials of the data are shown in Table 7.4. It is very clear that the associative data were overwhelmingly better than the experts at producing sentences that Korean students themselves would regard as being meaningful.

It is important to remember that the experts were themselves not Korean. They were persons who, as professional social scientists, studied the Korean language and culture. As well as they might have absorbed information about this culture, the data presented in Table 7.4 suggest that they had failed, as indeed we might expect, to become part of that culture. This comparison makes a very strong case for the use of associative data in providing an important tool in understanding a culture. Obviously, the associative norms contain information that the experts themselves do not know how to use intuitively.

Associations and Other Free Elicitation Techniques

There are, of course, elicitation techniques that are not, strictly speaking, associative in nature, but that, at the same time, exhibit many of the characteristics of associative responding. In fact, there is probably some kind of continuum extending from the structured interview to the method of continued association. An illustration is provided in a recent study by London and Lee (1977) of the Cultural Revolution in China. These investigators brought together a panel of 56 respondents who were refugees from the mainland residing in Taiwan. They compiled a list of 155 terms and expressions that had gained currency during the Cultural Revolution. The participants were instructed to tell, in writing, what each of these terms meant to them. These protocols were then translated into English by persons both familiar with the language and the events of the Cultural Revolution.

The analysis of the data strikingly resembles what one might accomplish with a test of free association. For example, two central concepts, that of *black line* (*hei-hsien*) and *red line* (*hung-hsien*) were perceived as being antonyms in the context of the Revolution. Fourteen respondents identified *red line* as the *Communist Party* itself. Sixteen panelists, including 6 illiterates (whose responses were oral) understood *red line* as the *proletarian road* to *Communism* (or *Mao's road*). The comparative weakness of the approach used by London and Lee is also evident in that a fair number of respondents, usually the illiterates, claimed not to have heard of or understand many of the concepts. The use of free-associational data undoubtedly would have helped determine whether that claim was correct or merely represented a disinclination of the respondents to respond to that particular item. Such a disinclination is a recurring problem in field research, and usually the more unstructured elicitation techniques of anthropologists are designed to try to get around it. When using a fixed format, as did London and Lee, such a problem is difficult to avoid. The associational technique is fixed, of course, but people, as all theorists from Freud on have remarked, are more likely to reveal their knowledge about the concept to which they are responding if they are associating than if they are asked a direct question or asked to produce that knowledge in the form of answers to questions.

London and Lee (1977), in their concluding remarks said: "The foregoing analyses demonstrate the possibilities of the empirical approach to areas of research in Sinology which have in the past relied mainly on nonempirical tools of scholarship" (p. 351). Without detracting from the usefulness of London and Lee's results, it is almost certainly the case that the use of an associative technique would have produced data less affected by subjective problems in analysis, more nearly free from inhibition in the expression of ideas, and more easily available for subsequent analysis by others interested in the problem. There will surely be situations in which nothing can replace the structured interview, but the determination of subjective meaning in a politically or culturally relevant semantic field is the kind of thing for which the method of continued association is unsurpassed. In any event, an important step would be the direct comparison of the results of an associative analysis with content analysis of the kind of data provided by London and Lee.

Finally, a point can be made in the context of the study by London and Lee, although it is more general than the particular issues to which the comparison above has been directed. The results of the elicitation techniques used by anthropologists, students of comparative government, and, indeed, by persons engaged in such things as clinical investigation, are not evaluated in the way in which psychometric or experimental psychologists are used to evaluating their data. Psychologists' attitudes are, in general, behavioral. Pencil and paper data, they argue, must predict some behavioral outcome. Such an attitude is a useful one and has served to eliminate from the repertoire of psychological testing many a device that, although perhaps possessing a certain face validity, has no real useful purpose. On the other hand, it does lead to problems. Often, so-called concurrent validity has a certain circularity or "boot-strap" characteristic to it. One psychological device is used to justify another. Partly, this is a problem associated with the difficulty of measuring appropriate behavior and partly with the fact that behavior is controlled by a variety of attitudes and situational constraints. The failure to predict behavior from a single attitude is a poor basis to draw conclusions about validity. Well-controlled studies of the predictability of behavior (see Mischel, 1968) characteristically show that even the best of devices exhibit low correlations with behavioral patterns. It would be foolish to expect field studies to do better. Although common sense might lead us to suppose, for example, that respondents with more negative views about *red line* would be more likely to try to leave China than those with positive views, a host of factors, both cognitive or subjective and external, would operate to make that particular (behavioral) prediction risky.

Anthropologists and the interpreters of the political and social aspects of culture are, far more than psychologists, likely to adopt a posture that might be labeled Verstehen psychology. The aim is to interpret or understand rather than to predict. In behavioral terms, such a Verständlich approach is to prepare for a range of possible outcomes — not to be surprised, as it were. As such, investigations of this kind have a kind of continuity with historical studies, rather than with those investigations that aim for some particular outcome.

We believe both postures to be useful, and they are certainly not mutually exclusive. Empiricism, pure and simple, in which the emphasis is entirely upon the acceptability of some predetermined hypothesis is useful where the outcome encompassed by that hypothesis is of overwhelming importance. However, the purely empirical approach of testing one possible outcome after another seldom leads to any overall pattern of results of the sort expected by the political analyst or the monitor of a social system. The associative method stands prepared to serve both Verständlich and behavioral approaches. Along with standardized pencil-and-paper measuring devices and such highly developed techniques as multidimensional scaling, the associative method should be a part of the battery of methods psychologists can be prepared to use in experimental settings or in psychometric research. On the other hand, it also provides us with a rich method for exploring the subjective nature of a culture. Here, the interpretative functions of the results are sufficient in themselves. They provide us with a portrait of a social entity, much as the classical, psychoanalytic use of free associations provides the therapist with the interpretative basis for proceeding with an analysis.

8

Problems in the Treatment of Data

In Chapter 2 we introduced the methods for treating data that have served for nearly all of data analyses we have presented thus far. However, at that time we indicated that these methods were intended to be flexible and subject to change depending upon the circumstances arising in some particular investigation. In this chapter we deal with possible variations in the treatment of data and some consequences of those variations.

WEIGHTING THE RESPONSES

Our first problem concerns the precise numbers given the weightings to associations at different rank orders of occurrence. In Chapter 2 we assigned those weights on the basis of a test—retest study. We argued that if the same persons are retested at some later date with the same words, dominant or salient responses ought to be repeated on the second testing more often than responses that are less salient. If the initial responses to a concept are more salient than later ones, they ought to be repeated on the second testing more often. We showed, with 21 persons being tested and then retested several weeks later on 32 words, that indeed earlier respones are more likely to be repeated on retesting. We used the percentages of recurrence from these data as a way of deriving empirical weights to assigned to responses. These were used in nearly all the response-score data presented later in the book.

It might be objected that other weighting schemes are possible and that the data upon which the original weighting was based was scanty. Both of these objections are sensible, and we intend to deal with them here. First of all, we would like to allude to the results of some repetitions we have performed of the test—retest study, and then we would like to point out an alternative approach to empirical weighting.

Repetitions of the Test—Retest Procedure

In the original weighting, we simply took the percentage of times responses at a given position were repeated in subsequent testings at any position. These percentages were rounded to a single digit, and these were used as weights assignable to responses occurring at the same positions. This test—retest procedure has been repeated several times with, as might be imagined, slightly different results on each occasion. The largest departure from the original weighting occurred for a sample of Chinese students in Hong Kong responding in Chinese. The weights derived from this study were based upon a set of 24 stimuli responded to by 23 subjects. These weights and the comparable original weights are presented in Table 8.1.

The percentage repetition upon second testing was lower for the Chinese students than for the original American sample (or for that matter any other sample we have tested). It decreased, as did the original American sample, with later positions, although not nearly so rapidly. The result is, if we were to use the Chinese data for assigning weights, that the weighting factor would be much less steep. Or, put another way, responses occurring in later positions would be relatively more prominent in the response-score distributions.

It is possible that the lower frequency of repetition has to do with the political nature of the stimuli for these Hong Kong residents. Table 8.2 shows, however, that there was little difference in stability of responses between politically sensitive and other kinds of stimuli. A more plausible reason for the lower frequency of repetition was the nature of the instructions and consequent responding in the Chinese language. Strictly speaking, there is no concept corresponding to the English (Indo-European) concept "word." Chinese subjects, therefore, were instructed to respond with single "concepts" or "phrases." The result was that the respondents wrote, in general, more highly developed responses than would respondents writing in English. Simply because of the great-

TABLE 8.1
Weights Derived from Original American Sample Compared with
Weights from Chinese Sample

	Order of Response											
Weights	*1*	*2*	*3*	*4*	*5*	*6*	*7*	*8*	*9*	*10*	*11*	*12*
American	6	5	4	3	3	3	3	2	2	1	1	1
Chinese	5	4	3	3	2	2	2	2	2	2	1	1

TABLE 8.2
Percentage Recurrence of Responses on
Retesting for Chinese Respondents

Stimulus	Percentage	Stimulus	Percentage
Liu Shao-ch'i	46	Commune	31
Mao Tse-tung	41	Nation	31
Family	40	War	30
Democracy	40	Equality	29
Freedom	35	Me	27
Japan	35	People	26
China	34	Law	26
Chairman	34	Capitalism	26
Cadre	34	Work	25
Class	33	Revolution	23
Communism	33	Peace	20
Politics	31	Authority	17

er number of characters involved in the longer phrases, it would be less likely that precisely the same concepts would be reproduced as answers a week later. There was, it turns out, a correlation of $-.178$ (not significant) between length of response and frequency of repetition. Although the correlation was in the right direction, its magnitude does not encourage us to accept simple length of response as the mediating factor in the lower repetition on the part of Chinese subjects.

The fact of the matter is that the explanation lies in subtle characteristics of the Chinese language, of which the length-of-response matter is only a superficial manifestation. Because (written) Chinese is a concept rather than a word (or phonetic) language, it allows the expression of complicated ideas in gnomic or aphoristic form. Something of the flavor of the ability of Chinese people to combine several words or phrases into a single concept is revealed in, by now, such familiar translated phrases as "gang of four." There is the genuine possibility that Chinese is a language even better adapted to the expression of complicated ideas by associations than are English and related languages that rely more heavily on syntax and morphology to convey meaning. It must almost certainly be the case that associations are less ambiguous in Chinese than in English, or, in any event, not much more ambiguous than fully developed expressions in the language.

An Alternative Weighting Scheme

Before examining some of the consequences of changing weights, we look at another alternative for arriving at a weighting scheme. Instead of considering test—retest repetitions, we could examine repetitions within a given testing ses-

TABLE 8.3
Proportion of Responses at Each Order of Emission Given
in Other Positions by Other Respondents

Position	Proportion	Standard Deviation	Weighting
1	.670	.089	7
2	.629	.071	6
3	.569	.134	6
4	.477	.081	5
5	.433	.071	4
6	.429	.119	4
7	.327	.070	3
8	.300	.125	3
9	.288	.107	3
10	.281	.145	3
11	.246	.188	2
12	.211	.294	2

sion. As we pointed out in Chapter 2, although it was not explicitly forbidden, almost no subjects duplicated responses during the 1-minute period allowed for continued association. Therefore, it might serve as a measure of the dominance of responses in a particular position to consider how often responses emitted by a particular individual were duplicated by responses emitted by other individuals at other positions.

Table 8.3 shows the proportion of responses at each of 12 positions in the order of responding and the resulting weights derived from an investigation of 50 words responded to by 50 University of Virginia undergraduates. The words were chosen to be representative of a wide variety of domains, including politics (*Nixon, liberal, Carter*, etc.), life styles (*work, gay, Led Zepplin*, etc.), emotions (*proud, fear*, etc.), personal relations (*mother, brother*, etc.). The weightings arrived at by this scheme are based upon the percentage of times responses given in a particular position were repeated in other positions. The resulting weightings are slightly higher. Evidently, agreement in responding is higher within sessions than across sessions, but the relations among the weights are virtually the same. Using these data instead of the original data to arrive at response scores would have produced only minor differences in the numerical results and no difference whatever in the pattern of results.

In general, then, idiosyncratic responses tend to appear late in the distribution of free associations, and those responses that reveal shared meaning appear early. The degree to which responses to a given stimulus are widely shared by the respondents provides another measure of the salience of the feature or features revealed by that response. We have made the assumption that the degree to which responses are shared is a measure of the salience, not only for the group, but in the particular mental representation of a typical respondent. For some individuals, of course, that assumption will be wrong. For some particular person, some idiosyncratic feature will dominate his or her conception of a theme and that assumption will be incorrect. However, the data in Table 8.3 reaffirm that idiosyncratic responding is rare in the first position. In fact, these data underestimate the lack of idiosyncratic responding, since the proportions in Table 8.3 do not take into account the duplication of responses by different individuals in the same position. The highest proportion of responses duplicated in other positions was for the concept *war*. It was .875. When we added the responses given in duplicate at that position but not responded to by others in other positions, the figure rose to .917. In short, very few responses in the first position to this stimulus were idiosyncratic, so our notion of mental representation applied to the average subject is here quite representative. Incidentally, the standard deviations for the proportion of repetitions, as noted in Table 8.3, were lower for the early positions than for the later ones. That means there is greater homogeneity in the lack of idiosyncratic responding across stimuli at the earlier positions than at the later ones.

All in all, despite the scanty data upon which the original weightings were based, there is little reason to change them for general purposes. As we shall note below, there might be some conceivable reasons for changing them, but there do not involve a change in our assumptions about the relation of dominance or salience in order of responding so much as they involve a change in perspective.

DATA FOR INDIVIDUALS

Within-Subject Correlations

In nearly all of our analyses thus far, we have ignored the within-subject correlations in patterns of responses. We have been, by and large, justified in so doing, because we have aimed at group or cultural rather than individual representations. As we have just noted, subjects tend on the average to duplicate one another's responses so long as the group is reasonably homogeneous, and we can make the assumption of assortative responding with little fear that it will distort the picture achieved for the group. However, almost any group will be heterogeneous in some respect. That is, some subjects will tend to agree with one another about some particular theme whereas others will not. Such a situation must happen where a group is divided in some attitude. Table 8.4 lists the responses to *government* of five subjects who gave only negative evaluative responses to *liberal* and five subjects who gave only positive evaluative responses to *liberal*. We have labeled these "liberal" and "conservative," respectively.

Although there was a surprising degree of duplication of responses between the liberals and conservatives, the differences were there. As we might expect,

TABLE 8.4
Responses of Five Liberal Subjects and Five Conservative Subjects
to *Government*

Liberal Responses	Score	Conservative Responses	Score
President	15	Carter	13
Federal	11	Job	13
Democratic	10	Structure	9
People	6	Sloppy	8
U.S.	6	President	6
Bureau	5	Federal	5
Policy	5	Foreign affairs	5
Spending	4	Autocracy	4
Senate	3	Sprawling	3
Congress	3	Bill of Rights	3
Helping	3	Monarchy	3
Red tape	3	Parliamentary	3
Father	3	De Gaulle	3
Economy	3	War	3
Upper class	3	Socialism	3
Society	3	Regulation	3
Action	3	Capital	3
Liquidate	3	Castro	3
Separate	3	Dishonest	3
Laws	3	Wasteful	3
Red tape	3	Control	3
Politics	3	Bureaucracy	3

helping, action, and *democratic* occurred to the liberals, whereas *sloppy, sprawling,* and *autocracy* occurred to the conservatives.

When the responses of a single subject to a group of stimuli were examined, it was clear that characteristic style often emerges. This is not surprising, for Moran and his associates (Moran, Mefford, & Kimble, 1969) as well as others have noted "idiodynamic" response sets that are consistent within subjects across stimuli and response sets. Something of the nature and pervasiveness of these styles of responding can be appreciated by comparing the distributions of a pair of subjects to items that generally elicit high affective scores. The pair of subjects chosen for Table 8.5 was chosen at random from the 50 Virginia students who responded to these items. One (No. 20-2) was a female; the other (No. 21-34), a male. The male subject in this case was the more consistently affective responder (and the affect was predominantly negative). The female subject only approached his degree of affectivity on responses to two stimuli, *abortion* and *war*. However, it was more than a difference in degree of affectivity. It was also the way in which affectivity was expressed. There were almost no epithets in the responses of the female subject, whereas such responses were very evident in the male subject.

TABLE 8.5
Comparison of the Responses Produced by Two Individuals Selected at
Random to Stimuli that Generally Produce High-Affectivity Scores

	Responses (in Order)		*Responses (in Order)*	
Stimuli	*Subject 21–34*		*Subject 20–1*	
Abortion	1. Murder	7. Women's lib	1. Fetus	7. Money
	2. Catholic	8. Illegal	2. Pill	8. Man
	3. Fetus	9. Salt	3. Birth Control	9. Woman
	4. Slime	10. Baby	4. Kill	10. D.C.
	5. Kill	11. Life	5. Psychology	11. Clinic
	6. Hate		6. Blood	12. Blacks
Carter	1. Jackass	7. Idiot	1. President	7. Kid
	2. Populist	8. Economy	2. Farmer	8. Jimmy
	3. Asshole	9. Taxes	3. Southerner	9. Decisive
	4. Liberal	10. Campaign	4. Smile	10. White House
	5. Peanut	11. Jimmy	5. Teeth	11. Congress
	6. Liar		6. Drawl	12. B-1 Bomber
Gay	1. Happy	6. Queer	1. Homosexual	6. Rights
	2. Cheerful	7. Orange juice	2. Lesbian	7. Anita Bryant
	3. Faggot	8. Gay rights	3. Happy	8. Sin
	4. Anita Bryant	9. Mike	4. Bar	9. Physical
	5. Warm	10. Closet queen	5. Queer	10. Effeminate
Liberal	1. Jerk	6. Knee jerk	1. Conservative	6. Democrat
	2. Commie	7. Conservative	2. Ideas	7. Views
	3. Pinko	8. Government	3. Free	8. Fast
	4. Carter	9. Cancer	4. Flippant	9. Jumps
	5. Pseudo	10. Fool	5. Carter	
Nixon	1. Crook	7. Dean	1. President	7. Coverup
	2. Fascist	8. Y.A.F.	2. Watergate	8. Pardon
	3. Pig	9. Liar	3. Old	9. Ford
	4. Watergate	10. Sick	4. D. Frost	10. Pat
	5. Agnew	11. Demented	5. Interview	11. Julie
	6. Haldeman	12. Pitiful	6. Tapes	12. Trisha
War	1. Peace	7. Nixon	1. Peace	7. Men
	2. Hate	8. World War II	2. Killing	8. Death
	3. Violence	9. Atomic	3. Destruction	9. Cannon
	4. Napalm	10. End	4. Bombs	10. Wounded
	5. Vietnam	11. Death	5. Aid	11. Fighting
	6. Kill		6. Cities	12. Weapons

Such striking differences between subjects were largely ignored in our group analysis. They were not just affective or emotional differences, for as we have noted before, affectivity can only be separated out of a whole series of responses. A given particular response is the result of the total operation of the cognitive and affective structure operating at the time it is produced. When we examined the response distributions of other subjects we found other, equally striking idiosyncratic modes of responding that were not affective in character. Some subjects simply knew more than others, and that greater knowledge about the themes embodied in the stimuli was evident in the kinds of responses they produced.

Other Treatments of Data for Individuals

Thus, by our emphasis upon the analysis of associations of groups rather than individuals, we do not mean to imply that associations of individuals are uninteresting or uninterpretable. It may well be the case that an interest in individual associations would cause us to change two more or less arbitrary features of our data analysis: (a) we may wish to abandon differential weighting of early responses, and (b) we may wish to extend the time and/or number of repetitions of the stimulus. In the first instance we should remember, however, that salience is a property of individual minds. Some features come more readily to mind than others, and this important property of subjective experience can only be ignored with deliberate awareness of the distortion to which it may lead. In the second instance, extension of opportunity for responding may well have its limits. There is no precise way to determine what those limits are; they would undoubtedly depend upon the circumstances of testing. However, one of us (Deese) has experimented with as many as 100 repetitions given to a single individual spread out over a month. With nearly 50 stimulus items examined in these observations, it is clear that repetition of responding soon becomes an overwhelming compulsion. The subject most extensively studied in this exploratory effort reported that a kind of satiation of meaning for the concepts being tested set in. This subjective sense of satiation accords with the nearly mechanical repetition of the same response that occurred later in the experiment. The response presents itself to the mind of the respondent with little sense of meaning or comprehension. Thus, it is by no means certain that simply extending the process of continued association will lead to an increasing proportion of new, idiosyncratic responses. This whole area needs exploration in the context of the study of personality and its relation to cognitive processes.

Dominance and affectivity are two general dimensions within which all the specific semantic features common to groups of individuals are organized. These characterize individual minds as well. Furthermore, individual minds are characterized by a third general dimension of uniqueness. The comparison in Table 8.5 shows that this dimension may be assessed, both in degree − the extent of the deviation from the average − and in the specific semantic features that characterize the deviation. Subject 21-34 is particularly interesting in the latter respect because the responses in Table 8.5 suggest that he cannot be easily characterized along the familiar liberal–conservative dimension. His responses to other simuli confirm this expectation. To *educated* he gave *intelligent, scholarly,* and *liberal*, among other responses. To *social security* he gave *necessary*; to *men, chauvinistic*; and to *women, liberate*.

Idiosyncratic Responses

These two subjects differed in the extent to which they produced unique responses. Subject 20-1 gave 115 unique responses out of a total of 401, or 28.7%, whereas Subject 21-34 gave 163 unique responses out of 374, or 43.6%. Both of these subjects are probably well above the average in this respect. It should also be pointed out that all but a very few of their unique responses are readily interpretable by an observer. Those that are not are, by and large, proper names. Thus, the overwhelming majority of idiosyncratic responses do not reflect totally private meanings. They can easily be interpreted by other individuals sharing the culture and background of the respondents. Many of these responses reveal meanings that are low in salience for most people, but it is possible that some are purely linguistic and would appropriately be combined into large domains. This result causes us to revise our procedures somewhat. In nearly all of the analyses presented earlier, idiosyncratic responses were eliminated from consideration. Although including them would affect the results for the typical stimulus very much, one could imagine situations in which some considerable information relevant to a domain might be in question. Or, even more likely, the affective dominance scores might change considerably as the result of the inclusion of unique responses. The concept *Nixon*, for example, elicited many epithets. There were a few repetitions – *crook* occurred ten times for a total response score of 46 – but most of them were unique. However, these would never enter into the total score by our rule of excluding idiosyncratic responses. The result of excluding them would be that the (almost exclusively negative) affective dominance index for *Nixon* would be reduced from -.232 to -.171.

In short, although we have purposefully adopted a strategy that eliminates idiosyncratic responses in cross-cultural studies, they may sometimes be of use. Idiosyncratic responses have been eliminated in large-scale comparative studies because these studies require hundreds of thousands of responses and automatic data processing. Their inclusion would be impractical and generally would add little. The choice to include or exclude them must be made in the light of the purpose of the investigation.

LIMITATIONS OF THE ASSOCIATIVE METHOD

Finally, we need to say a word about some of the more important limitations of the associative method. Because of the inherent ambiguity of associations, they do not always tell us with precision about persons' knowledge. They can tell us about the kinds of knowledge individuals possess – what in general they know about some concept – but they do not give us an exhaustive account of their knowledge nor do they give us exact accounts of a particular piece of knowledge possessed by individuals. Both Johnson (1964) and Verplanck (personal communication) have experimented with using associations as tests of knowledge. Johnson made use of free associations in assessing the knowledge high school students had of basic concepts in physics; Verplanck used a kind of controlled association test as a replacement for a multiple-choice test in introductory psychology. Both were able to demonstrate the validity of their methods, but at the same time it cannot be said that they were able to demonstrate any particular advantage to the associative method in general as a means of assessing some well-targeted piece of information. Johnson pointed out, however, that the use of associations enables one to determine how people think about some concept, whether in fact the particularized knowledge embedded in, for example, knowing the basic relations among terms in energy is a part of the person's ordinary, daily thought processes. This is particularly the case because the setting for associative testing does not provide the kind of settings expected for revealing knowledge as such. Therefore, what knowledge is revealed in an associative test is apt to be that which is assimilated into the day-to-day cognitive processes of the person being tested and which occurs spontaneously without self-consciousness.

In this connection we should point out that we have avoided any of the available varieties of controlled association because we have reason to believe that they seriously increase the degree of self-conscious monitoring and because they present a view of the subjective world that is distorted by the filter of the specialized instructions. Category norms (e.g., Battig & Montague, 1969), for example, provide specialized information about one cognitive process, namely, the development of semantic classes, and as such have their uses. But the implied hierarchical organization of mental processes comes from the experimenters and their instructions to their respondents, not from the respondents themselves.

In summary, we do not regard any of the procedures we have developed as absolutely fixed but rather as the most appropriate procedures for the purpose of comparing and contrasting groups of persons who come from different cultures or who might be expected to reflect different social outlooks. Almost any of the procedures or treatment of data could be changed for some special purpose; . . . the notions of dominance, affinity, and affectivity are central to our view of the nature of the subjective world, and we would expect them to be represented somewhere in the procedures and analysis of data. Our use of free associations in the first place is based upon arguments originally made by Galton and elaborated as an integral part of psychoanalytic theory by Freud. It is the freedom from external constraint and censorious processes that provide the advantage of the associative method in the first place. The use of continued rather than discrete associations is one important innovation added, and it has its origins in earlier use. It serves to provide a richer data base, compared to the usually meager information offered by single responses. The primary response, in discrete association, often serves to hide responses that are almost as close to the surface of consciousness as the primary response when we are aroused by some stimulus to reveal our subjective view of the concept encoded in the stimulus.

Therefore, once again, except for highly specialized purposes, we believe that the method of continued rather than discrete associations is the method of choice when the purpose of the investigation is to determine the subjective meaning of some set of stimuli. The precise length of time (or number of responses) allowed each respondent is not something that can be fixed by theory or by some general methodological rule. It is clear, however, that the early responses are the more important ones, so far as the significant features of subjective meaning are concerned, and, furthermore, it is possible that a kind of semantic satiation may set in if we require too many respones to a given stimulus. The method of continued association, however, coupled to a scoring system that gives weight to the salient responses, provides the most sensitive and flexible elicitation technique for investigating subjective meaning yet devised.

9 Representing Subjective Meaning

The purpose of this final chapter is to explain the nature of our conception of subjective meaning. This is partly a matter, as it turns out, of making explicit a certain conception of the uses of theory in psychology. It is also a matter of making explicit the expected uses of associative data in the study of subjective meaning.

CURRENT PSYCHOLOGICAL STUDIES OF MEANING

Experimental Work

Much of the contemporary psychological concern with meaning has centered in the experimental study of cognition and information processing. It has devolved around matters of semantic storage, encoding and retrieval, the formation and comprehension of sentences and stories, and, to a lesser degree, problem solving. The major concern has been to formulate theories of semantic storage that account for or describe the results of experiments in which people remember word lists, sentences, stories, etc., or experiments in which the subjects are required to perform certain operations upon the materials, such as deciding whether statements are true or false. These matters have not been our concern, and, therefore, it should not be surprising that it is possible for us to ignore most of the features possessed by these theories. It simply is not relevant to our purpose to be concerned with whether linguistic information is stored in a kind of network of propositions or in some other way. Furthermore, since the cognitive and information-processing theories are essentially process models, the experiments have not turned upon matters of general psychological interest, but upon small differences in contrived situations. Often, these depend upon the use of reaction time to assess the complexity of the assumed process. Our interests, on the other hand, turn upon large-scale social-psychological matters, and the characterization of individuals and groups.

Measurement of Meaning

Another, perhaps less active contemporary concern with semantics has been with the measurement of meaning. Here, the major emphasis appears to be upon scaling devices and data-reduction techniques that take advantage of internal consistencies. The investigations are intended to represent the most important features or dimensions of meaning possessed by some group of words. The methods themselves — e.g., sorting, similarity scaling, — tend to define the theory. The general approach is not limited to the representation of the subjective lexicon. Extensions have been aimed at examining general features of consciousness or mental representation (e.g., Shepard & Metzler, 1971). Although this work is closer in spirit and intent to the investigations reported here than the experimental studies, there are two critical features that set our investigations apart from work in this tradition. One of these features is largely procedural, but the other is both procedural and conceptual.

We have already, in Chapter 7, commented upon the procedural difference. At that point we characterized it as being principally a difference between a method in which the meaning of a word is established without context, as in the associational method, and a method in which the meaning of a word is established within the context of the particular group of words used on a particular occasion, as in the various scaling and sorting methods. This most important procedural difference has two consequences. One is that the characterization of the meaning of any one word by a contextual method is inevitably dependent upon the other words with which it is compared or sorted. The other is that, in general, these contextual methods are limited in the number of words that can be processed in any single investigation. Those methods, such as multidimensional similarity scaling, that depend upon a comparison of every item with every other item are particularly limited because the number of observations quickly becomes too large as words are added, and the treatment of the data exceeds the practical capacity of even very large computers for extended samples of words.

The important conceptual difference is provided by the fact that the contextual methods all imply a particular theory as to the organization of the subjective lexicon. Each method implies its own theory. Unfortunately, there is little except our intuitive knowledge of words, almost no theory of semantic organization independent of the psychological methods, to tell us which method is appropriate to a given set of words. It is perfectly possible for people to sort a set of words into a hierarchical tree and then imply a spatial organization for the same words by making judgments of similarity. The data-analysis techniques are capable of arriving at two very different and perhaps incompatible representations for the same words.

It need not be assumed that one or both of the representations are "wrong." It is simply that they are different. Each represents application of a different semantic operation. The semantic operations themselves may well reflect the cognitive organization of the human mind (Deese, 1969; Fillenbaum & Rapoport, 1971), and as such it is not any more unreasonable than to find human beings harboring contradictory beliefs. Certain operations, of course, may be contradicted by the semantic relations among the words themselves, and, for these the application of certain operations would be inappropriate. As we have pointed out before, it is nonsense to ask how a fish and a minnow are similar. It may also be nonsense to ask people to classify into various groups red, green, blue, yellow, orange, purple, etc. So, application of one or another of these methods is often dependent upon our knowledge of lexical relations and our intuitions about the words we are investigating. A glance at an ordinary dictionary shows that it mixes semantic operations in a thoroughly satisfactory way. Perhaps, for purely lexical purposes — even subjective lexical purposes — we cannot improve upon a good dictionary. But, as we have seen by now, subjective meaning is more than this.

The Associative Method

Like the contextual methods, the associative methods establish the meaning of a word by considering its relation with other words. However, the relation for the contextual methods is always among words preselected by the investigator. The relation for the associative methods is between a word selected by the investigator and the word produced freely by the subject. This is a fundamental distinction, and one responsible for the flexibility of the associative method.

In an earlier approach (Deese, 1965), overlapping distributions of associations were treated as a measure of similarity and subjected to factor analysis in order to yield a spatial representation of the relations among words. This use, of course, parallels treatment of data from the various contextual methods and, in particular, those methods based upon multidimensional scaling. However, as we pointed out in Chapter 2, overlapping distributions of associations, which we now prefer to describe as affinity measures, are not necessarily based upon the relation of similarity but upon any and all relations that mediate responses to stimuli in free association. As such, affinity scores have no simple interpretation. They do not measure degree of similarity or any other particular relation. They simply sum any and all relations revealed by associations. If A and B have a higher affinity score than A and C, it means that A and B have more salient relations than A and C. But it does not specify what those relations are.

THE PRESENT APPROACH

We have, at various places in this book, pointed out that we have not intended to develop a process model. We have simply assumed that associative relations between stimulus and response represent a relation that can be interpreted as a statement of some sort. How these relations are stored or generated is not something that enters into the treatment and interpretation of data we have gathered. In fact, it just may be the case that no particular process model may be established as the most plausible one simply by testing various aspects of models in psychological experiments. The major accomplishment of process models thus far is in their ability to make explicit the kinds and complexity of human abilities we are able to assume in our theories. They serve as measures of the competence we are willing to ascribe to human beings.

We do not operate in the absence of theory, however, as that term is generally understood. Any enterprise that goes beyond the most limited reporting of raw data contains some theory, explicit or implicit. A great deal intervenes between our raw data and the presentation of facts, and much of that constitutes theory. Much of the remainder is based upon general knowledge. We are able to draw upon the facts and theories of anthropologists, linguists, political theorists, and psychologists working in other fields with other methods. Whenever we have drawn upon such general knowledge in the interpretation of data, we have tried to point it out. More than this, however, it is necessary to point out how our choice of methods and analysis of data depend upon our view of the nature of the subjective representational process. The easiest way to do that is with a recapitulation and exposition of the assumptions made in the first chapter.

The Subjective Representational Process

We said in Chapter 1 that associations made implicit statements linking the stimulus and the response. Perhaps this is obvious, but the long history of treating associations simply as stimulus—response connections makes it necessary that we be absolutely explicit about this. We make no particular claim about how these statements arise. There are strong reasons for believing that the subjective representational system is not in the form of language itself, but it is almost impossible to avoid presenting the results of that system in the form of statements, as when we point out that the response *polite* to *educated* is a way of saying that politeness is an attribute of an educated person.

Currently, there are many different ways available of representing the kind of relations implicit in linguistic statements, associations, images, and other products of the subjective representational system. There does not seem to be any overwhelmingly strong reason for picking one of these over the other, particularly in the context of our use of associations to probe subjective culture and cultural differences.

We need hardly point out in this connection that associations involving nonverbal terms, either as stimuli or responses or both, can also be interpreted as or translated into statements of some sort. Once again, this does not commit us to the implication that the subjective representational system itself is propositional, i.e., consists of some set of labeled relations as those described in HAM (Anderson & Bower, 1973).

Because, by the large, syntax is missing in associations, there is an unavoidable degree of ambiguity in the assignment of particular statements to a given association. The ambiguity is present to varying degrees and may be paralleled by the degree of ambiguity in the assignment of particular statements to a given association. The association *President* to *Carter* may, with almost no ambiguity, be taken to be equivalent to the statement: "Mr. Carter is President." The association *Congress* to *Carter* is considerably more ambiguous. For a particular person it may mean: "Congress and Carter are opposed;" or, perhaps, "Congress dominates Carter." In this case, we should formulate our statement at the most general level possible, perhaps as: "There is a relation between Mr. Carter and Congress."

It is clear that there is no simple and automatic way to interpret associations. We must use our knowledge of a particular culture and of a particular group of people to infer from associations what kinds of things people are saying. We have already pointed out that the response *liberal* to the name of a politician may be pejorative when given by some one of reactionary leanings and at the same time be affectively positive when given by someone of liberal persuasion.

The relations implicit in associations provide an account of psychological meaning. They reveal the dominance of particular concepts in the subjective representational system, the salience of particular relations, the affinities among relations, and the degree of affectivity associated with particular concepts. Subjective meaning includes beliefs, attitudes, feelings, and any other psychologically characterizable reaction to external objects as stimuli. Perhaps this is another reason for avoiding the process models of cognitive psychology, for they might well force us to differentiate among those things that reveal knowledge, those that reveal emotional reactions, and those that reveal beliefs and opinions.

Dominance

As we have just noted, the representational system is characterized by dominance. Some concepts are more important to a given individual or to a given group of individuals. Whole domains in the subjective representation may likewise be more important than other domains, and components of those domains will vary in importance. The dominance of a theme or domain may be inferred from or revealed by the rate at which persons are able to produce associations to that theme or to themes within that domain. We noted in Chapter 2 that the relation between associative rate and dominance must be taken in context. A taboo concept or theme may yield, because of suppression of responses, a low dominance score. Yet it may be central to the subjective representation of individuals within a certain culture.

The number of associations weighted by position provides a measure of dominance for individuals. Because of the weighting, differences in dominance for individuals are smaller than if the number of responses simply were tabulated. For groups, dominance requires us to sum all responses weighted by position. Once again, the weighting by position, makes group differences in dominance relatively smaller than if we had simply summed responses.

The notion of dominance is stated in the most general way possible, however, because it is sometimes convenient or appropriate to modify weighting schemes, etc. In Chapter 2 we outlined an empirically derived method for assigning weights to associations, and we mainly made use of that weighting in the subsequent chapters. In Chapter 8, however, we pointed out the consequences of changing weights. Although they are not large in the overall pattern of results, they do exist. In short, we do not claim to have an explicit and detailed theory to connect our particular choices of weighting, nor do we believe that any general weighting scheme could be particularly justified by an accord between the theory that might occasion it and the data.

The notion of salience among the associative relations is as useful as the generality of associative relations themselves. Some beliefs are about matters more central to a given person's life than are others. Beliefs about matters of varying centrality are held with varying degrees of conviction. Some knowledge is better structured and more easily retrieved than other knowledge. There is no point in assuming that any single quantitative index applied to data will have universal validity because: (a) any particular scheme would probably be wrong for some purpose; (b) the purposes to which the assumed relation are put do not justify the precision implied by some fixed and, in theory, at least, hypothetically derived expression; and (c) the "real" relations may vary with some as yet undiscovered or undiscoverable characteristic of people.

Affinity

The representational system is characterized by affinal relations. An index of affinity provides a measure of the extent to which concepts form significant relations with other concepts. Certain themes or concepts have a kind of centrality, and such a theme has richer relations with the other concepts in that domain than the others. Furthermore, domains themselves will differ in the extent to which there are rich relations among the themes. It is this richness in affinity that provides one of the most important characteristics of the subjective representational system and its susceptibility to external influence. If, in a particular culture, a given domain is characterized by rich relations of affinity, no matter what the semantic character of those relations, the structure will be resistant to change. If, on the other hand, a concept exists more or less in isolation, some new information about the concept will be influential: It will organize new affinal relations.

An example of a theme that occupies a central role in one culture and not another is provided by *rice* in the Korean culture compared with American culture. For Koreans *rice* is not only related to various other themes in the domain of *food* but also to themes in the domains of *economics* and *poverty*. Rice is the main Korean food, and it plays a central role in the Korean economy. Therefore, it is not surprising that *rice* produces an affinal index for the Koreans approximately twice that for Americans in the context of the domains of *economy* and *food*. Furthermore, *poverty* and *hungry* are more intimately related for Koreans than for Americans. Consider the interrelations of *hungry, rice, food, to eat* with *poor, money*, and *beggar*. For the American sample, the major relations of *hungry* are with *food* and *to eat*. The average affinity scores relating these two concepts and *hungry* for the Americans was 420, whereas for the Koreans it was 314. Americans are more likely than the Koreans to think of being *hungry* as a relatively benign state in which one seeks out food. On the other hand, the relations of *hungry* with *poor, money*, and *beggar* are greater for the Koreans than for the Americans. The average affinity index for the Koreans relating these concepts to *hungry* was 269, while for the Americans it was 152. The affinity of *hungry* and *beggar* was particularly high for the Koreans.

It is sometimes instructive to examine the responses in common that produce affinal relations. These tell us not only that there is a relation but some of the semantic properties of the relation. For example, consider the affinal relations between *law* and *freedom* for Black students compared with White students. It is not surprising that the White students exhibit a higher affinal index between these two concepts than do the Black students (190 compared with 127), but an examination of the particular responses in common produces some interesting results. The Black and White students agree that *law* and *freedom* are both *good*, deal with *people*, are things we *need*, and are both associated with *peace* and *justice*. Furthermore, *law* appears to be essential for *freedom* but more for White students than Black students. Where these students differ is in only two responses, *country* and *God*. Both of these occur with moderate scores in the Black and White distributions for *freedom*, but they occur to *law* only for Whites.

Of course, more specialized searches for relations are possible. It may be desirable, for example, to examine affinal relations for entire domains, or to limit the examination to some special class of responses, such as descriptors.

Finally, it may be interesting to limit the search to within-individual distribu-tions. While such an approach lies outside of the scope of associative group analysis, one of the authors (Deese) has been using affinal relations to investigate attitudes by limiting the search for relations to overlapping responses within in-dividuals. The *Carter-Nixon* example, mentioned in the preceding chapter pro-vides a case in point. Although there was some considerable overlap in the descriptors applied to both *Carter* and *Nixon*, the overlap almost entirely dis-appears when we consider only within-person relations. The people who re-garded *Nixon* as *smart, cautious*, or *corrupt* were not the same people who re-garded *Carter* as *smart, cautious*, and *corrupt*.

In summary, then, affinal relations provide two kinds of information about subjective meaning. First, indices of affinity tell us how closely related concepts are, how they form themselves into clusters. It is a matter of interest, for exam-ple, that *religious* and *familial* themes may be closely related in one culture and not in others. Or, if one is looking to influence attitudes in some group or cul-ture, examining the affinal relations will reveal whether or not one is dealing with an isolated theme or with a structure of many related themes.

Affectivity

Affectivity is a critical dimension of subjective meaning because subjective mean-ing implies an ego-centered perspective. The nature of that perspective is re-vealed in belief, opinion, and attitude. Beliefs, opinions, and attitudes concern different things and concern different kinds of knowledge. The only thing all beliefs, opinions, and attitudes have in common is the perspective of the individ-ual responding, as evident in the evaluative dimension of affectivity. Affectivity, as we have often noted, is inherently a part of the structure of subjective mean-ing. All of our conceptual categories express affectivity to some degree. Since, as Deese (1973) pointed out, an astonishing number of our abstractions are in the form of spatial metaphors, space itself tends to acquire a metaphorical affective quality. Such an abstraction as "hierarchical representation," for ex-ample, is couched in a language suffused with potential affective judgment: "Higher nodes," "dominate," "lower nodes." Except for abstract symbol systems, such as mathematics, human thinking appears to be inextricably bound with affectivity. Because the perspective of the ego provides a reason for select-ing, focusing, and movement of subjective experience, it is almost essential, in any treatment of that experience through associations, to consider affectivity and how it is expressed.

Association based measures of attitudes and evaluations inform without ask-ing sensitive personal questions about the extent to which people like or dislike certain themes, events, ideas, or people. Furthermore, as we saw in Chapter 6, associative methods not only yield measures of attitudes, they can also reveal the salient information upon which the attitudes are based.

ASSOCIATIONS AS AN ELICITATION TECHNIQUE

Comparison with Other Elicitation Techniques

Free associations, of course, provide but one of many elicitation techniques used in the study of subjective culture, of belief and attitudes, and a word placing them in the general framework of elicitation techniques is in order. Psychologists, even though they tend not to use the term, have been more concerned than anthropologists with the use of predetermined and standardized elicitation techniques. The whole enterprise of attitude measurement has grown up with the development of sophisticated standardized techniques and methods for the treatment of data that go with them. These go hand in hand with the concern for the application of carefully designed sampling techniques. Sociologists have shared this concern with sampling and, to almost the same extent, with standardized elicitation techniques, although they have tended more often to use a set of questions rather than the specialized scaling techniques more favored by psychologists. Anthropologists have more often relied on field training to provide flexibility and cultural specificity in eliciting information. Since anthropologists are often interested in eliciting information that is taboo or otherwise difficult to obtain, they often must interpret the information they receive from their informants in the light of the contextual knowledge they have about the culture. In anthropological reasearch, there must be a great deal of interpretation of casual remarks.

Free-associational techniques sit somewhere in the middle of this continuum. They are fixed in format, and everyone must respond to the same items (or at least to a preselected set of items) for them to work. On the other hand, the results can be subjected to a variety of interpretations. People who know the group or the culture being studied well can supply information that makes sense out of associations that may otherwise appear to be incomprehensible. Furthermore, associations also lend themselves to objective and statistical treatment.

Furthermore, as we have remarked in several places, associations are almost completely context free. They do not determine the pattern of responses from an informant as do other techniques, even things like unstructured interviews. In free associations, we do not ask our respondents: "What do you think of X?" or "How do you evaluate Y?" Instead, we simply let the respondents' own interpretation of the stimulus as a concept in their own mind determine the outcome. That is why dominance or salience is such an important feature of free-associational analysis. We want to know what, in the familiar metaphor, is closest to the surface of the person's mind when faced with a particular concept or theme.

Use in Market Research

Such information is potentially of value in market research. We have gathered no data that are, strictly speaking, relevant to marketing problems (e.g., brand names as stimuli), but an item similar in interest may help illustrate the potential use of associations in market research. *Led Zepplin* is the name of a rock band popular in the late 60s and early 70s. We used the term as a stimulus item in the set of 50 concepts presented to students at the University of Virginia who were described in the last chapter. It was clear that our respondents were knowledgeable about the group. *Heavy metal, acid rock*, and *hard rock* were all responses that could be taken as (more or less accurate) descriptors of style. Specific titles were mentioned, of which the most common was *Stairway to Heaven*. Real interest centers in the evaluative responses. These, from undergraduate students, surprised us by being heavily negative. Evaluative responses were 13% of the total, and the evaluative-dominance index was $-.10$. This is despite the fact that we eliminated such responses as *freaky* from the negative evaluation set on the grounds that they might not be negative in this particular context.

Why the evaluation was heavily negative becomes clear when other responses are examined. These students regarded the *Led Zepplin* group as (a) out of date and (b) associated with their own early adolescence, both of which they clearly regard as being against the group. Thus, associations to this concept established three facts: (a) the respondents knew a fair amount about the concept; (b) they were primarily negative in their evaluation of it; (c) the reason for the negative evaluation was that tastes had changed. Now it might be argued that the same information could have been obtained from a three-item questionnaire. That may well be the case. On the other hand, if we wanted to know exactly those characteristics (*loud, capitalism* (!), *slick, harsh, crass, flashy, twang, high voices*, etc.) responsible for the evaluation, we would probably have had to add innumerable questions. If we want the data to reflect the characteristics of the respondents without the imposition of organization supplied by the investigator, the associative method is the method of choice.

Strengths of Associative Group Analysis

It is precisely in this respect that one of the principal strengths of the associative method and particularly of what we have called associative-group analysis lies. It provides an opportunity for respondents to present their own subjective world, as they organize it, in their own words. Its disadvantage comes from its comparative lack of focus. If an investigator wants a specific piece of information (e.g., "Should President Ford have pardoned Mr. Nixon?"), it would be wasteful to employ the associative method.

However, one of the most important general principles underlying recent research in cognitive processes (e.g., see Mandler, 1975) is that people cannot give an account of their own mental processes. Thus, to ask a point-blank question such as, "Why do you like X?" invites rationalization. It is the most significant feature of free associations, as we pointed out in the first chapter and shall have demonstrated shortly, that they are, more than any other verbal process, free from the kinds of rationalizing that serve to screen us from our own interpretations of our motives, feelings, and beliefs.

To make this point concrete, a word needs to be said about free-associational data compared with data of a similar sort that asks respondents to make full use of the structural (i.e., grammatical) characteristics of language. We have collected a small amount of data that enables us to compare free associations with situations in which persons are asked to respond by composing a sentence that includes the stimulus word. And, we have also asked people to write a short essay about the stimulus concept.

In the first instance, we asked 10 University of Virginia undergraduates to write 10 sentences on each of 10 stimulus themes. The test was made as similar to an association test as possible. The words were listed at the head of each line on which the subjects were to write their sentences. However, instead of allowing 1 minute to produce as many responses as possible (averaging for the Virginia students approximately eight responses per item), the subjects were introduced to the stimulus only once and asked to write a short essay about it "saying anything you think is significant about the concept." In this case, 4 minutes was allowed for each item, and subjects responded only once to each item.

In a first analysis of these data, the contentive as opposed to functional words were pulled out of the sentences. From these, personal sentential complements ("I think that . . .") were deleted. The remaining respones were listed in the form of an associative distribution. It should be noted that several of our subjects took the sentence-writing task to be a kind of free-associational test, with the result that sentences of the sort, "X makes me think of Y," occurred repeatedly. We assigned weights, such as those in the continued free-association task, to words based upon the order of the sentence in which they occurred. Thus, words from the first sentence were assigned a weighting of six, words in the second sentence a weighting of five, etc. The result, of course, was not the same as assigning weights to associations, because, for one thing, we used a fixed number sentences, and, for another, there would sometimes be more than one content word in a sentence. For the essays, we tried several weighting schemes but, as noted in the following discussion, abandoned them. The 10 stimuli, all drawn from the set of 50 words given to University of Virginia undergradutes in an associative task described in Chapter 8, were: *girl, Carter, mother, liberal, boy, abortion, Nixon, gay, father,* and *serious.*

The correlations between the response-score distributions of associatons to these words and response-score distributions based upon the content of the sentences in the sentence task averaged, after Z transformations, .482. This is lower than typical test–retest correlations on associations, but it is higher than many cross-group correlations. It is clear that many of the words used in the sentences also turn up in associations, although the particular frequencies vary. The lowest correlation was for *girl* (.217), and it appears to be the result of a strong definitional characteristic to the sentences ("A girl is a female child") and the fact that no one used the word *boy* in any of the sentences in response to *girl*. The highest correlation occurred for Nixon (.632). The epithets and negative evaluative responses in the associations agreed well with the characterizations for this item in the very commonly given sentence of a "is" or "is a" variety.

There was really no way to compare the essay data with free-associational distributions. The reason is, in part, because the essays were clearly artificial and constricted. They were short, and they were usually dominated by a single theme.

The fact of the matter is that associations provide information not available in either the sentence or the essay task. Sentences tend to be descriptive, and the significant attitudinal and motivational components of meaning are simply missing from them. As one subject put it after we had explained the purpose of the sentence task: "It's hard to express your feelings in sentences." The incompleteness of meaning derived from sentences explains the low correlations between sentences and associations.

In the first chapter we relied very heavily upon the view of the process of free association developed from its use in psychoanalysis. The great virtue of associations, from the point of view of psychoanalysis, is their ability to escape the censorious processes that develop when we are asked to respond to direct questions. Undoubtedly, the special conditions of the psychoanalytic session – the darkened room, the relaxed posture, the mood created by the analyst, etc. – have much to do with the uninhibited nature of the responses in the psychoanalytic session, but, as we have pointed out repeatedly in the book, some of that freedom from inhibition comes from the peculiar nature of the process itself.

One place where that freedom from inhibition is evident is in the comparison of the free associations and the sentences. Strangely enough, it is not so obvious in the stimuli that would appear to be sensitive to or involve high degree of affectivity (e.g., *gay*, *Nixon*) but in those stimuli that appear to be ordinary and to have only mild affect associated with them (*boy*, *girl*, etc.). Not only do our male subjects, in responding to *girl* as a stimulus to free association produce many more responses centering on *sex* than they do in forming sentences, they also produce such interesting and potentially revealing responses as *lonely* and *molester*. One male subject, whose responses to other stimuli strongly suggested an overt homosexual orientation produced the following responses to *girl*: *femininity, lesbian, vagina, sex, subordinate, acceptance, housewife, kids, sadness, mother*. Nothing like that set of respones occurred anywhere in the sentences. The stimulus *boy* produced from female subjects such responses as *sexless, penis, hate, need approval, want* and other responses that had no parallel in the sentential data. The same stimulus from male subjects produced such responses as *sad, used to be, penis, no pubic hairs, love*, and *derogatory*. The latter did occur in the sentences (*"Boy* is a *derogatory* term applied to *Black males* in the *South."*) Incidentally, the word *South* also occurred in the free associations to *boy*, although not from the same subject giving *derogatory*.

Although, without additional information, either in the form of associations to related responses or in the form of information about the persons responding, it is impossible to place a certain interpretation upon the significance of these responses, they do suggest affectivity in areas that tend to be either suppressed or do not occur at all when subjects are asked to respond to questions or to produce sentences in response to concepts.

Meaning Not Necessarily Linguistic

Just what it is about the process of free association that makes for such potentially revealing sets of responses is a matter of some concern. We may take it as a starting point that some or all of the cognitive processes responsible for the production of language are themselves not linguistic. This is, by now, a very common view (e.g., Fodor, Bever, & Garrett, 1974; Pylyshyn, 1973), and several models of linguistic—cognitive processes are based upon the assumption that the essential meaning of a segment of language about to be produced is generated in some nonlinguistic form ("mentalise" is the term used by Fodor et al.) and then transformed into the language of the speaker. Without accepting the details of such a notion, we may accept the general idea that at least features — and probably important features — of ideas expressed by sentences or associations occur in nonlinguistic form first. The transformation of an idea, or essential features of it, into grammatically well-developed language requires an appreciable time. There is excellent evidence[1] to show that, even in the middle of a sentence, alternative modes of expression may be considered, with one or more modes being rejected or (rarely) coming together in a kind of a grammatical blend. In short, the process of transformation, although itself not available to conscious experience, is consciously monitored and may be altered by instructions from some executive function. There is reason to believe that the monitoring may be well ahead of actual production, for internal evidence in certain disfluencies suggests that speakers are altering a sequence they are working on in an effort to avoid some word or phrase that will not appear for a while.

---

[1]One of us (Deese) is currently engaged in a project designed to discover as much as can be learned about the production of language from studying the characteristic disfluencies in production. Using a variety of inferential techniques, it is possible to show that what is coming up later influences what is being produced at the moment. For word-to-word relations, most such relations are internal to sentences and phrases, although general plans intrude to alter early sentences in anticipation of sentences coming later.

Associations Not Monitored

Here, we believe, lies one of the principal reasons why associations are more nearly free from censorious control than are responses that are embedded in the full grammatical form of language. They occur more rapidly and offer less chance for monitoring to occur. The transformation from idea into language is quicker and easier. As was recognized almost from the beginning of empirical research on free associations, monitoring does occur, and for that reason reaction time in free association has often been used as an indicator of emotional arousal; the assumption being that a stimulus arouses affect, and, perhaps as a result, a "dangerous" response must be edited out and replaced by an inoffensive one. However, even so, many responses that might be embarrassing or revealing to a subject do escape, for it is another characteristic of free association that the propositions or statements behind them are not fully realized. Not being fully realized means that the full implications of the assertion implied by the association are not made available to conscious monitoring before the response occurs.

Such a view implies that there are degrees of freedom from inhibitory processes in association. It may well be the case that a person, particularly when writing and not subject to immediate scrutiny by the experimenter, may well decide that a particular response is revealing but go ahead and put it down anyway, taking refuge in the ambiguity of the association. It is possible for a subject to produce misleading and false associations, of course, but the task is so intellectually demanding that when faced with the necessity of producing a whole series of associations, subjects who wish to hide their thoughts from or mislead the investigator usually resort to some predetermined set, such as using klang associates or replacing the stimulus, mentally, with a phonetically related word. Such patterns, of course, are easy to detect, as are mistakes in reading the stimulus, etc.

Thus, we claim no special or mysterious powers for association, but merely a degree of freedom from conscious editing of responses that is bought at the expense of the ambiguity inherent in a linguistic production that makes only the most primitive use of the grammatical apparatus of a language. Associations are not pipelines to unconscious processes or windows directly on the subjective experience of persons. They provide us with one view into the person's interior world, one that all the evidence suggests is less distorted than that provided by any other standardized elicitation technique available for mass testing, but that still is altered by the demands of responding. We can obtain some idea of how that interior world is organized by studying the relations among responses in free association, although once again we must be aware of the distortion introduced by the testing process, by the very fact, for example, that the results are embedded in language. Even the artful psychoanalyst must be wary in the use of detailed probing and entertain hypotheses only with great skepticism about the relations in the subjective mind of the patient.

THE USES OF ASSOCIATIVE ANALYSIS

Finally, we shall say a word in summary about the various uses to which associative analysis of group data may be put. In a sense, this entire book is about the uses of word associations. Because the book has concentrated upon the use of associations to determine particular subjective meanings, however, we have neglected another important aspect of associations, namely employing them to determine the structure of the totality of a subjective culture. While a detailed treatment of such large scale uses of associations is beyond the cope of this volume, we would not provide a complete account of the potential of associative data if we did not at least mention them.

There have been several studies making use of associative data to provide information about some sizeable portion of a subjective culture. For example, Lee Young-Ho (1972) has used word associations in his study of social-economic beliefs about modernization among Korean legislators and trade unionists. Bobrow, Chan, and Kringen (1977) have compared, over a large domain of social-political beliefs, Chinese samples from Hong Kong with immigrants from the People's Republic of China. Szalay and Pecjack (in press) have done a comparative analysis of American and Slovenian political beliefs.

The comparative analysis of subjective cultures or belief systems as a whole is a larger problem. Studies of this sort may involve the examination of as many as twenty cultural domains having high priority and the use of as many as 200 stimulus words. The strategy in such studies is described at length by Szalay and Maday (1973). A large cultural analysis may be based upon hundreds of thousands of reactions. Such an analysis, which we have not discussed in this volume, may require the analysis of dominant trends within the framework of a single, large stimulus-response matrix. Some of the analyses reported in Chapter 3 are based upon data from such global studies of the subjective culture. Currently, one of us (Szalay) is engaged in a comparative analysis of American and Arab (Jordanian and Egyptian) subjective cultures as well as a similar analysis of American and Iranian cultures.

The purpose of such studies is to help establish understanding among national groups. They serve to show American users how their understanding of key concepts — indeed whole domains — compares with various other cultural groups. These comparative analyses provide the basis for a kind of language instruction which is oriented towards communication. While learning a new language, people may refer to such analyses to learn about the culture and its people's characteristic ways of thinking as well.

Finally, several studies of subjective meaning through associations have been useful in applications to social learning. Brent (1970), for example, has used an associative group analysis to evaluate the effects of encounter group experiences in a federal reformatory, while Kelly, Dockett, Farber and West (1972) have used it to study police-community relations. In Chapter 4 we examined the data from a study of the psychocultural distance between American and Filipino enlisted men in the United States Navy. An important part of that study was an examination of the process of acculturation on the part of the Filipinos with years of service in the Navy. In Chapter 5 we saw that associations could be used to evaluate the influence of such communicative devices as films.

The range of application of these and similar analyses is limitless. We have mainly pointed to cross-cultural and attitudinal comparisons, but market research, studies of the subjective representation of the physical and social environments provide other possibilities. The use of associative data in helping us to understand the mental processes of others who have not had our experiences and who do not share our prejudices and values has barely begun. We hope that the illustrative examples presented in this book will open up vistas in cross-cultural comparisons. The exploitation and refinement of a technique that, basically, is as old as empirical psychology itself has just begun.

References

Aarsleff, H. The history of linguistics and Professor Chomsky. *Language,* 1970, *46,* 570–585.

Anderson, J. R., & Bower, G. H. *Human associative memory.* Washington, D.C.: Winston, 1973.

Battig, W. F., & Montague, W. E. Category norms for verbal items in 56 categories: A replication and extension of the Connecticut norms. *Journal of Experimental Psychology,* 1969, *80,* 1–46.

Bauer, R. A. The psychology of the Soviet middle elite: Two case studies. In C. Kluckhohn, H. A. Murray, & D. M. Schneider (Eds.), *Personality in nature, society and culture.* New York: Knopf, 1959.

Bauer, R. A., Inkeles, A., & Kluckhohn, C. *How the Soviet System Works.* New York: Vintage Press, 1956.

Benedict, R. *The chrysanthemum and the sword.* Boston: Houghton Mifflin, 1946.

Bloomfield, L. *Language.* New York: Holt, 1933.

Bobrow, D., Chan, S., & Kringen, J. Understanding how others treat crises. *International Studies Quarterly,* 1977, *21,* 199–222.

Bousfield, W. A., Whitmarsh, G. A., & Berkowitz, H. Partial response identities in associative clustering. *Journal of General Psychology,* 1960, *63,* 233–238.

Bousfield, W. A., Whitmarsh, G. A., & Danick, J. J. Partial response identities in verbal generalization. *Psychological Reports,* 1958, *4,* 703–713.

Brent, J. Changes in frame of reference among staff participants in staff-inmate encounter groups in a federal reformatory. Washington, D.C. Bureau of Prisons, 1970.

Brotsky, S. J., & Linton, M. L. The test-retest reliability of free association norms. Psychonomic Science, 1967, *8,* 425–426.

Brown, R. W. Discussion. *American Anthropologist,* Special Issue, 1964, *66,* 288–301.

Burling, R. Cognition and componential analysis: God's truth or hocus-pocus? *American Anthropologist,* 1964, *66,* 20–38.

Casagrande, J. B., & Hale, K. L. Semantic relationships in Papago folk-definitions. *Studies in Southwestern Linguistics.* The Hague, Mouton, 1967.

Clark, H. H. On the use and meaning of prepositions. *Journal of Verbal Learning and Verbal Behavior,* 1968, *7,* 421–431.

Clark, H. H. Word associations and linguistic theory. In J. Lyons (Ed.), *New horizons in linguistics.* Baltimore, Md.: Penguin, 1970.

Cofer, C. N. Associative commonality and ranked similarity of certain words from Haagen's list. *Psychological Reports,* 1957, *3,* 603–606.

Conklin, H. C. Ethnogenealogical method. In W. H. Goodenough (Ed.), *Explorations in cultural anthropology.* New York: McGraw-Hill, 1964.

Cramer, P. *Word associations.* New York: Academic Press, 1968.

Creelman, M. B. *The experimental investigation of meaning: A review of the literature.* New York: Springer, 1966.

Dalrymple-Alford, E. C., & Aamiry, A. Word associations in bi-linguals. *Psychonomic Science,* 1970, *21,* 319–320.

D'Andrade, R. G., Quinn, N., Nerlove, S. B., & Romney, A. K. Categories of disease in American-English and Mexican-Spanish. In A. K. Romney, R. Shepard, & S. B. Nerlove (Eds.), *Theory and applications in the behavioral sciences.* New York: Academic Press, 1972.

Deese, J. Form-class and the determinants of association. *Journal of Verbal Learning and Verbal Behavior,* 1962, *1,* 79–84.

Deese, J. On the structure of associative meaning. *Psychological Review,* 1963, *63,* 161–175.

Deese, J. *The structure of associations in language and thought.* Baltimore, Md.: Johns Hopkins Press, 1965.

Deese, J. Conceptual categories in the study of content. In G. Gerbner (Ed.), *Communication and content.* New York: Wiley, 1969.

Deese, J. Cognitive structure and affect in language. In P. Pliner, L. Krames, & T. Alloway (Eds.), *Communication and affect.* New York: Academic Press, 1973.

Deese, J. Mind and metaphor: A commentary. *New Literary History,* 1975, *6,* 211–217.

Deese, J. Semantics, categorization and meaning. In E. C. Carterette & M. P. Friedman (Eds.), *Handbook of perception* (Vol. VII). New York: Academic Press, 1976.

Deese, J., & Hamilton, H. W. Marking and propositional effects in associations to compounds. *American Journal of Psychology,* 1974, *87,* 1–15.

Deno, S. L., Johnson, P. E., & Jenkins, J. R. Associative similarity of words and pictures. *AV Communication Review,* 1968, *16,* 280–286.

Ebbinghaus, H. *Über das Gedachtnis.* Leipzig: Duncker & Humbolt, 1885.

Fillenbaum, S., & Rapoport, A. *Structures in the subjective lexicon.* New York: Academic Press, 1971.

Fishbein, M. A. A consideration of beliefs and their role in attitude measurement. In M. A. Fishbein (Ed.), *Readings in attitude theory and measurement.* New York: Wiley, 1967.

Fodor, J. A., Bever, T. G., & Garrett, M. F. *The psychology of language.* New York: McGraw-Hill, 1974.

Freud, S. *Collected papers.* London: Hogarth, 1924.

Galton, F. Psychometric experiments. *Brain,* 1880, *2,* 149–162.

Garskof, B. E., & Houston, J. P. Measurement of verbal relatedness: An idiographic approach. *Psychological Review,* 1963, *70,* 277–288.

Gegoski, W. L., & Riegel, K. F. A study of one year stability of the Michigan free and restricted association norms. *Psychonomic Science,* 1967, *8,* 427–428.

Goodenough, W. H. Componential analysis and the study of meaning. *Language,* 1956, *32,* 195–216.

Goodenough, W. H. Yankee kinship terminology: A problem in componential analysis. *American Anthropologist* (Special Issue), 1965, *67,* 259–287.

Gorer, G., & Rickman, J. *The people of great Russia.* London: Crosset Press, 1949.

Greenberg, J. H. *Language Universals.* The Hague: Mouton, 1966.

Hallowell, A. T. Ojibwa personality and acculturation. In S. Tax (Ed.), *Selected Papers of the Twenty Ninth International Congress of Americanists,* 1949, *7,* 105–112.

Harvey, O., Hunt, D., & Schroeder, H. *Conceptual systems and personality organization.* New York: Wiley, 1961.

Henley, N. A psychological study of the semantics of animal terms. *Journal of Verbal Learning and Verbal Behavior,* 1969, *8,* 176–184.

Horvath, W. J. A stochastic model for word association tests. *Psychological Review,* 1963, *70,* 361–364.

Howes, D. On the relation between the probability of a word as an association and in general linguistic usage. *Journal of Abnormal and Social Psychology,* 1957, *54,* 75–85.

Hull, C. L. Knowledge and purpose as habit mechanisms. *Psychological Review,* 1930, *37,* 511-525.

Inkeles, A., & Bauer, R. A. *The Soviet citizen.* Cambridge, Mass.: Harvard University Press, 1961.

Inkeles, A., & Levinson, J. National character: The study of modal personality and sociocultural systems. In G. Lindzey (Ed.), *Handbook of social psychology,* (Vol. II). Cambridge, Mass.: Addison-Wesley, 1954.

Johnson, P. E. Associative meaning of concepts in physics. *Journal of Educational Psychology,* 1964, *55,* 125–127.

Jones, E. E., & Sigall, H. The bogus pipeline: A new method for measuring affect and attitude. *Psychological Bulletin,* 1971, *76,* 349–364.

Jung, C. G. *Studies in word association* (M. D. Eder, trans.). New York: Moffat Yard, 1919.

Karwoski, T. F., Odbert, H. S., & Osgood, C. E. Studies in synesthetic thinking: II. The role of form in visual response to music. *Journal of General Psychology,* 1942, *26,* 199–222.

Katz, J. J. *Semantic theory.* New York: Harper & Row, 1972.

Katz, J. J., & Fodor, J. A. The structure of semantic theory. *Language,* 1963, *39,* 170–210.

Kelly, G. *The psychology of personal constructs.* New York: Norton, 1963.

Kelly, R., Dockett, D., Farber, M., & West, G. The pilot project: A description and assessment of police-community relations. Washington, D.C.: American Institute for Research, 1972.

Keppel, G., & Strand, B. Z. Free associations to the primary response and other responses selected from the Palermo-Jenkins norms. In L. Postman & G. Keppel (Eds.), *Norms of word associations.* New York: Academic Press, 1970.

Kintsch, W. *The representation of meaning in memory.* Hillsdale, N.J. Lawrence Erlbaum Associates, 1974.

Kluckhohn, F. R. Culture and behavior. In G. Lindzey (Ed.), *Handbook of social psychology.* Cambridge, Mass.: Addison-Wesley, 1954.

Kolers, P. A. Interlingual word associations. *Journal of Verbal Learning and Verbal Behavior,* 1963, *2,* 291–300.

Laffal, J. *A concept dictionary of English.* Essex, Conn.: Gallery Press, 1973.

Laffal, J. A., & Feldman, S. The structure of single word and continuous word associations. *Journal of Verbal Learning and Verbal Behavior,* 1962, *1,* 54–61.

Lambert, W. E., Havelka, J., and Crosby, C. The influence of language acquisition contexts on bilingualism. *Journal of Abnormal and Social Psychology,* 1958, *56,* 239–244.

Lee Hahn-been. Korea: Time changes and administration. Honolulu, Ha.: East-West Center, 1968.

Lee Young-Ho. Economic growth vs. political development. *Korea Journal,* 1972, *12,* 5–11.

London, I. D., & Lee, T. L. Socio/psycholinguistics of the cultural revolution: *Psychological Reports,* 1977, *40,* 343–356.

Lounsbury, F. G. A semantic analysis of the Pawnee kinship usage. Language, 1956, 32, 158–194.

Lyons, J. Structural semantics: An analysis of part of the vocabulary of Plato. Oxford: Blackwell, 1963.

Mackenzie, B. D. Measuring the strength, structure, and reliability of free associations. Psychological Bulletin, 1972, 77, 438–445.

Mandler, G. Mind and emotion. New York: Wiley, 1975.

Marshall, G. R., & Cofer, C. N. Single word free association norms for 328 responses from the Connecticut Cultural Norms for verbal items in categories. In L. Postman & G. Keppel, (Eds.), Norms of word association. New York: Academic Press, 1970.

McNeill, D. A. A study of word associations. Journal of Verbal Learning and Verbal Behavior, 1966, 5, 548–557.

Mead, M. And keep your powder dry: An anthropologist looks at America. New York: Morrow, 1942.

Metzger, D., & Williams, G. E. Procedures and results in the study of native categories: Tzeltal firewood. American Anthropologist, 1966, 68, 389–407.

Miller, G. A. Psycholinguistic approaches to the study of communication. In D. L. Aron (Ed.), Journeys in science: Small steps – Great strides. Albuquerque, N.M.: University of New Mexico Press, 1967.

Mischel, W. Personality and assessment, New York: Wiley, 1968.

Moran, L. J., Mefford, R. B., & Kimble, J. P. Idiodynamic sets in word associations. Psychological Monographs, 1965, 78, (No. 579).

Noble, C. E. An analysis of meaning. Psychological Review, 1952, 59, 421–430.

Ogden, C. K. Opposition: A linguistic and psychological analysis. Bloomington, Ind.: Indiana University Press, 1967. (originally published 1932).

Ogden, C. K., & Richards, I. A. The meaning of meaning. New York: Harcourt, Brace, 1956. (Originally published, 1923).

Osgood, C. E. The nature and measurement of meaning. Psychological Bulletin, 1952, 49, 197–237.

Osgood, C. E. Semantic differential technique in the comparative study of cultures. American Anthropoligist, 1964, 56, 171–200.

Ostrom, T. M. The bogus pipeline: A new ignis fatuus? Psychological Bulletin, 1973, 79, 252–259.

Pollio, H. R. Composition of associative clusters. Journal of Experimental Psychology, 1964, 67, 199–208.

Pollio, H. R. The structural basis of word association behavior. The Hague, Mouton, 1966.

Postman, L. L., & Keppel, G. Norms of word association. New York: Academic Press, 1970.

Pylyshyn, Z. W. What the mind's eye tells the mind's brain. Psychological Bulletin, 1973, 80, 1–24.

Ramsey, J. O., & Case, B. Attitude measurement and the linear model. Psychological Bulletin, 1970, 74, 185–192.

Ray, S. Korean-Japan relations. Koreana Quarterly, 1965, 6, No. 2.

Riesman, D. The Lonely Crowd. New Haven: Yale University Press, 1950.

Rokeach, M. The open and closed mind. New York: Basic Books, 1960.

Romney, A. K., & D'Andrade, R. G. Cognitive aspects of English kin terms. American Anthropologist, 1964, 66, 146–170.

Rozin, P., & Gleitman, L. R. The structure and acquisition of reading. II: The reading process and the acquisition of the alphabetic principle. In A. S. Reber & D. L. Scarborough (Eds.), Towards a psychology of reading. Hillsdale, N.J.: Lawrence Erlbaum Associates, 1977.

Russell, W. A., & Jenkins, J. J. The complete Minnesota norms for responses to 100 words from the Kent-Rosanoff Word Association Test. Minneapolis, Minn.: University of Minnesota, 1954.

Shepard, R. N., & Metzler, J. Mental rotation of three dimensional objects. *Science,* 1971, *171,* 701–703.

Shugar, G., & Gepner-Wiecko, K. Effect of language structures on associative responses to word equivalents in the language: A cross-linguistic comparison of word associations in Polish and English. *Polish Psychological Bulletin,* 1971, *2,* 99–105.

Sigmund, P. Ideologies of the developing nations. New York: Frederick Preager, 1963.

Siipola, E., Walker, W. N., & Colb, O. Task attitude in word association, projective and non-projective. *Journal of Personality,* 1955, *23,* 441–459.

Stefflre, V., Reich, P., & McClaren-Stefflre, M. Some eliciting and componential procedures for descriptive semantics. In P. Kay (Ed.), *Explorations in mathematical anthropology.* Cambridge, Mass.: M.I.T. Press, 1971.

Szalay, L. B. *Eine psychologisch-semantosche Untersuchung von Zeitworten.* Ph.D. Dissertation. University of Vienna, 1961.

Szalay, L. B., & Bryson, J. A. Measurement of psychocultural distance: A comparison of American Blacks and Whites. *Journal of Personality and Social Psychology,* 1973, *26,* 166–177.

Szalay, L. B., & Bryson, J. A. *Filipinos in the Navy: Service, international relations and cultural adaptation.* Washington, D.C.: American Institutes for Research, 1977.

Szalay, L. B., Bryson, J. A., and West, G. *Ethnic-racial attitudes, images and behavior by verbal associations.* Technical Report. Kensington, Md.: American Institutes for Research, 1973.

Szalay, L. B., Lysne, D., & Bryson, J. A. Designing and testing cogent communications. *Journal of Cross Cultural Psychology,* 1972, *3,* 247–258.

Szalay, L. B., & Maday, B. Verbal associations in the analysis of subjective culture. *Current Anthropology,* 1973, *14,* 33–50.

Szalay, L. B., Moon, W. T., Lysne, D., & Bryson, J. *Communication lexicon on three South Korean audiences: Social, national and motivational domains.* Technical Report. Kensington, Md.: American Institutes for Research, 1971.

Szalay, L. B., Moon, W. T., & Bryson, J. *Communication lexicon on three South Korean audiences: Family education and international relations domains.* Technical Report. American Institutes for Research, 1973.

Szalay, L. B., & Pecjack, V. Comparative analysis of U.S. and Slovenian social and political frames of reference. In L. Seaton (Ed.), *Political anthropology.* The Hague, Mouton (in press).

Szalay, L. B., Williams, R. E., Bryson, J. A., & West, G. *Priorities, meanings, and psychocultural distance of Black, White, and Spanish-American groups.* Technical Report. Kensington, Md.: American Institutes for Research, 1976.

Szalay, L. B.&Windle, C. Relative influence of linguistic vs. cultural factors on free verbal associations. *Psychological Reports,* 1968, *22,* 43–51.

Szalay, L. B., Windle, C., & Lysne, D. Attitude measurement by free verbal associations. *Journal of Social Psychology,* 1970, *82,* 43–55.

Taylor, I. How are words from two languages organized in bilingual memory? *Canadian Journal of Psychology,* 1971, *25,* 228–240.

Terwilliger, R. F. Free association patterns and familiarity as predictors of affect. *Journal of General Psychology,* 1964, *70,* 3–12.

Terwilliger, R. F. *Meaning and mind: A study in the psychology of language.* New York: Oxford University Press, 1968.

Thompson, C. E. *Thompson modification of the Thematic Apperception Test.* Cambridge, Mass.: Harvard University Press, 1949.

Torgerson, W. S. Multidimensional scaling of similarity. *Psychometrika,* 1965, *30,* 379–393.

Triandis, H. C. Cultural influences upon cognitive processes. In L. Berkowitz (Ed.), *Advances in experimental social psychology* (Vol. 1). New York: Academic Press, 1964.

Triandis, H. C., & Vassiliou, V. *Componential analysis of subjective culture.* Urbana, Ill.: University of Illinois, 1967.

Triandis, H. C., Vassiliou, V., & Nassiakou, M. Three cross-cultural studies of subjective culture. *Journal of Personality and Social Psychology (Monograph Supplement),* 1968, *8,* (No. 4).

Tversky, A. Features of similarity. *Psychological Review,* 1977, *84,* 327–352.

Underwood, B. J. Verbal learning in the educative process. *Harvard Educational Review,* 1959, *29,* 107–117.

Verplanck, W. S. Personal communication, 1965.

Wallace, A. F. C. Mazeway resynthesis: A bio-cultural theory of religious inspiration. *Transactions of the New York Academy of Science,* 1956, *18,* 626–638.

Watson, J. B. *Psychology from the standpoint of the behaviorist.* Philadelphia: Lippincott, 1924.

Whorf, B. L. *Language, thought, and reality.* Cambridge, Mass.: M.I.T. Press, 1956.

Wispé, L. G. Physiological need, verbal frequency, and word association. *Journal of Abnormal and Social Psychology,* 1954, *49,* 229–234.

Woodworth, R. S., & Schlosberg, H. *Experimental psychology* (2nd ed.). New York: Holt, 1954.

Wundt, W. Uber psycholigsche Methoden. *Philosphische Studien,* 1883, *1,* 1–38.

Index